HANDBOOK OF RECORD STORAGE AND SPACE MANAGEMENT

New Titles from QUORUM BOOKS

The Export-Import Bank at Work: Promotional Financing in the Public Sector
Jordan Jay Hillman

Supply-Side Economics in the 1980s: Conference Proceedings
*Federal Reserve Bank of Atlanta and Emory University Law and
Economics Center, Sponsors*

Deregulation and Environmental Quality: The Use of Tax Policy to Control
Pollution in North America and Western Europe
Craig E. Reese

Danger: Marketing Researcher at Work
Terry Haller

OPEC, the Petroleum Industry, and United States Energy Policy
Arabinda Ghosh

Corporate Internal Affairs: A Corporate and Securities Law Perspective
Marc I. Steinberg

International Pharmaceutical Marketing
Suresh B. Pradhan

Social Costs in Modern Society: A Qualitative and Quantitative Assessment
John E. Ullmann, editor

Animal Law
David S. Favre and Murray Loring

Competing for Capital in the '80s: An Investor Relations Approach
Bruce W. Marcus

The International Law of Pollution: Protecting the Global Environment in a
World of Sovereign States
Allen L. Springer

Statistical Concepts for Attorneys: A Reference Guide
Wayne C. Curtis

HANDBOOK OF RECORD STORAGE AND SPACE MANAGEMENT

C. Peter Waegemann

Q **Quorum Books**

Westport, Connecticut
London, England

Library of Congress Cataloging in Publication Data

Waegemann, C. Peter.
   Handbook of record storage and space management.

   Bibliography: p.
   Includes index.
   1. Records—Management.   I. Title.
HF5736.W18   1983   651.5'3   83-3442
ISBN: 0-89930-017-0 (lib. bdg.)

Library of Congress Catalog Card Number: 83-3442
ISBN: 0-89930-017-0

First published in 1983 by Quorum Books

Greenwood Press
A division of Congressional Information Service, Inc.
88 Post Road West
Westport, Connecticut 06881

Printed in the United States of America

10 9 8 7 6 5 4 3 2 1

To my wife Yvonne and to my son Marc

CONTENTS

    Systems Overview   71
    In-house Microfilming Versus Contract Filming   76
    Storage of Microfilm   77
    Preservation Policy   81
    Equipment   85
    Legality of Microfilm   89

5. Computerization   93

    What Computers Can Do for Records Management   93
    Equipment Selection   105
    Information Carriers   111

6. The Future of Records Management   119

    Future Technology and Its Impact   119
    What to Do   121

    Appendix A Manufacturers Index   129
    Appendix B Professional Publications and Associations   133
    Appendix C Recommended Reading   135
    Index   137

ILLUSTRATIONS

FIGURES

TABLE

PREFACE

Records management is at a crossroads. Since the times of Gutenberg, when the written word was first reproduced mechanically, the question of handling and storing documents has become ever more important.

Twentieth-century photocopying technology has increased the volume of documents tremendously. As records managers run out of space in the records room, a professional evaluation of equipment, space, and alternatives is needed.

This book is written to aid in perpetual evaluation, in planning new record systems, as well as in reorganizations. It is intended for the records manager, the administrator, and the person who plans systems of microfilm, plans, X-ray films, paper documents, or any other information carrier, as well as anyone else concerned with records and their storage.

In the preparation of this book, an important question was how much basic information to include. I avoided filing techniques, records management techniques, and other standard information readily available. The emphasis of this book, therefore, is on consumer advocacy, space planning, and equipment selection.

Information media and products are compared according to cost and efficiency. My list of companies cannot claim to be complete; however, I did try to include every company and product I came across, and I would like to apologize if there is a company in any part of the country I missed.

Because cost containment is a major demand in our time, cost formulas are offered for storage systems. In the area of cost management, every records manager should be aware of alternatives and the effects of certain procedures and equipment on a department's budget.

Microfilm, as the best alternative to space shortage, is described for the records manager who has not started microfilming yet but is considering conversion to microfilm. The experienced microfilm manager will find subjects like the preservation of microfilm and the cost sections of interest.

What is in the future for records management? Is hard copy going to be replaced? And, if so, when and how? These are the questions I am trying to answer for the records manager in order to prepare him or her for the future.

This handbook analyzes professional issues, particularly with regard to information systems management, prepares the records manager for computerization, and describes word processing and computerized record trace systems. The discussion of consumer advocacy issues in regard to equipment selection should provide valuable help, particularly in the purchase of computer terminals.

The future of records managers depends on how they will find their place in the organization of information management systems. This book will try to point out how to understand these systems and records management's opportunities and will offer guidelines for records management's future professional obligations.

HANDBOOK OF RECORD STORAGE AND SPACE MANAGEMENT

1

PLANNING AND EVALUATING HARD COPY SYSTEMS

VOLUME PLANNING FOR EXISTING SYSTEMS

The first step in planning and/or evaluating a new or existing record system is to establish the system's volume. In existing systems this can be done by counting and measuring the records. However, counting is not recommended. The fact that a record volume consists of 10,000 files does not mean much for space planning purposes because records vary in thickness.

The professional way to establish the volume of a record system is to measure its volume in linear filing inches (LFIs) or linear filing feet (LFFs), 1 linear filing foot equaling 12 linear filing inches. To do this, measure the length of your documents as they are "in line" in cabinets, on shelves, or in any other kind of housing. The four-drawer file has individual drawers approximately 25 inches long each, so after allowing for block and drawer fronts, the volume of a total file cabinet would be 100 LFIs (4 × 25 = 100). A standard six-compartment lateral (shelf) file may be 30, 36, or 42 inches wide. If it is 36 inches wide, it contains 216 (6 × 36) LFIs of records. In applications where shelves have different levels of record density, an average has to be established. If a shelf or drawer is empty, it is not included in the volume count but is added to the listing of space available for expansion.

To establish the overall volume of a record department, add up all LFIs. Various filing systems in the department that do not interact in their indexing or function should be listed separately (i.e., folders and microfiches). Additional space should be planned for the future. The space required for future expansion depends on the retention schedule and on the increase in paperwork and documentation due to increased activity. If no data are available on such increases, an expansion factor of at least 25 percent should be used.

VOLUME PLANNING FOR A NEW OPERATION

When a new system is planned, there are obviously no records to count or filing inches to measure. This may be at the beginning of a new program or administrative process, be it that new government legislation requires a new department with a new record system or that a new commercial venture is started for which records will have to be kept. If a new building is planned, the volume can be established by looking at the anticipated activities. How many encounters, applications, policies, and procedures are expected per year or per month? How many pieces of documents will be created (1) in an average case and (2) in a special case? What correspondence can be expected during and after the processing period?

Estimates of the total number of expected documents (usually sheets of paper) will provide the first data base for space planning. To this estimate one has to add the thickness of containers, that is, the space taken up by folder covers and other document containers. Then the number of expected documents can be converted into space requirements. Different conversion figures have to be used depending on the anticipated number of pages per record.

For thin folders, 1,800-2,000 sheets of paper represent 1 LFF, or 12 LFIs. When folders reach an average thickness of 40 pages, covers take up proportionately less space. This means that approximately 2,500 pieces of paper will create 1 LFF. By dividing the number of anticipated documents into the conversion factor, one can determine how many LFFs are expected. Now we can go one step further and translate the expected number of LFFs into guidelnes for how much space is required by multiplying LFFs by the appropriate space efficiency factor.[1]

For instance, a new operation is expected to create 20 documents in a normal case and up to 60 documents in a special case, and the department anticipates up to 100 cases per month. The ratio of standard cases to special cases is two to one. By computing the total number of documents (39,600) and dividing that number by 2,500, a planning figure of 15.8 LFFs is determined. The records are to be kept for seven years. By adding 25 percent for adjustment and expansion, we end up with approximately 138.25 LFFs (15.8 × 1.25 × 7 = 138.25). Let's say we plan to place these cabinets with center aisles, that is, so that file cabinets are arranged on both sides of an aisle. If four-drawer, letter-size cabinets are used, the space required is approximately 135.49 square feet (138.25 × .98). If seven-tier lateral shelving is used in a single row along the wall, for instance, 69.12 square feet is required (138.25 × .50 = 69.12). Of course, I would recommend a discretionary figure of ± 20 percent with these figures. Also, a decision on the equipment should not be made on space considerations alone. Activity considerations are equally important. Hundreds of thousands of dollars have been wasted on highly space-efficient equipment that does not take into account the requirements of accessibility for an active file.

RETENTION POLICY

The retention period is one of the main criteria for planning a filing system. To determine how long records should be kept requires an examination of their value at various points of storage. Documents are certainly important while they are active. But how important are they after six months, one year, two years, five years? Or is it necessary to keep these records permanently? Looking at the type of information stored in the record system and the value of that information after its period of high activity can give us a feeling for the required retention period. Then there are legal requirements, over which the records manager usually has no control. In many cases the retention policy is established by the management of the organization. Here a records manager may be able to influence the policy directly or at least to influence the decision makers on that policy.

Retention periods can be divided into four categories: active information, that is, information that is not worth keeping, such as bulk mail announcements; short-term storage, up to three years; medium-term storage, up to seven to ten years; and long-term storage, over ten years. Of course, the retention period begins at the time that the work process on a given record is completed or settled. The following list gives various types of records and the period in years of their retention/authority.*

Record	Retention in years
Accession list	P
Accident report	30 AT
Accounts payable invoice	3
Accounts payable ledger/register	3-10
Accounts receivable ledger	2-10
Acknowledgment	WU
Acquisition record	6 AC-P
Adverse action file	4 AC
Advertising activity report	5
Advertising inquiry received	1 after response
Advertising mail received	0 AC
Affirmative action program	1 or WU
Aircraft operation/maintenance	50-P
Aircraft order document	2-10
Announcements, bulletin notices	0 AC

*AA, after audit; AC, after completion (end of active time period of file); AT, after termination (end of inactive time period of file); AV, after visit or discharge; C, current; MD, management discretion; P, permanent; Sl, depending on individual state limitation; WU, while useful, until superseded.

Record	Retention in years
Annual report/statement (published, certified)	P
Application: Personnel	
Nonemployee	MD
Employee	3 AT
Appraisal for buildings, plant, or property	50-P
Attendance record (Time Card)	2-7
Audit reports: government, internal, public	50-P
Audit work paper	3
Authorization for expenditures	3 AC
Authorization of approval	WU
Authorization to issue securities	6 AC-P
Balance sheet (audited)	P
Balance sheet (working)	AA
Bank deposit book/slip	2
Bank statement	2-6
Bill of material/substitutions	15
Bill of lading/waybill	2 AC
Blueprint/map (copy of masters)	MD
Bond	P
Broker's statement	6
Budget/cost record	3-5
Building permit	10 AC
Calibration (equipment/instrument)	15
Capital asset record	3 AC
Cash book/journal	3-10
Cash receipt record	7
Checks (canceled):	
Register	20-P
General	20-P
Dividend	6
Payroll	2-3
Taxes	6
Claims (against company):	
Group (life/hospital)	6 AC
Vehicle accident	2 AC
Any workman's compensation	6 AC
Product liability	10-P

Record	Retention in years
Claims (against others):	
Loss/damage in transit	2-6 AC
Classified document (Record)	2-10 AC
Cleared employee file/list	WU
Commission record (bonus, etc.)	6
Conflict of interest	2 AT
Constitution and bylaws	P
Consolidation records	6 AC-P
Contract:	
Employee	6-10 AT
Construction	3-6 AC
Advertising	3 AC
Customer (commercial)	3-10 AC
Government	3-6 AT
Reproduction (agents and distributors)	3 AC
Union	3 AC
Vendor	3 AC
Negotiated, bailment, change	P
Copyright record	P
Corporate tax record by IRS	75
Correspondence:	
Executive	P
General	5
Marketing/sales	3
Cost accounting record:	
Cost production and job summary	3
Cost report and statement	3
Labor distribution record	3
Price record	3
Counseling record	3
Courier authorization	2
Customer credit record	1-3 AC
Customer report	6-P
Credit union record:	
Employee	4 AT
Articles of incorporation	P
Ledger	P

Record	Retention in years
Damage report	3-6 AC
Debit memo/purchase copy	WU
Deduction authorization	2 AC
Deed/abstract	10 AC
Delivery report	3
Depreciation/fixed assets:	
Insignificant, short-life assets	3
Major, long-life equipment	P
Development study/marketing	P
Directive/policy/procedure	50-P
Directory and mailing change	WU
Disability and sick benefits	6 AC
Discrimination charges	3-4 AC
Dividend check	6
Dividend register	P
Drawing/artwork/layout:	
Advertising	MD-10
Engineering master	10-P
Earnings register: employee	P
Easement:	
Right of way	10 AC-P
Water rights	10 AC
Education/training record	10 AT
Election record (corporate)	P
Emergency condition report	50-P
Employee official personnel file:	
Hourly	4 AT
Salaried (Nonexempt)	4 AT
Salaried (Exempt)	6 AT
Employee badge/key record	2-5 AT
Employee case file police record	3-5 AT
Engineering record:	
Drawing	20-P
Notebook	20-P
Product design record	20-P
Research record	20-P

Record	Retention in years
Entertainment, gift, gratuity	3
Exception notice	WU
Expense report:	
Department	3
Employee	7-10
Travel	3
Export declaration	3
Facilities' check file (safety, guards, etc.)	1-3
Fidelity bond for employees	10 AC
Financial statements:	
Certified	P
Periodic	2
Fingerprints (security and employees)	10 AT
Fire and theft protection program	50-P
Forecast/estimate	5-10
Formula (engineering, etc.)	20-P
Franchise agreement	15 AC-P
Freight bill	3 AC
Freight claim	3 AC
Garnishment/attachment (personnel)	3AC
General ledger	P
General administrative records:	
Advertising literature	WU
Application for credit	1-5
Application for employment	1-5
Circular	WU
Collection letter	1-7
Note of appreciation	WU
Note of transfer, promotion	WU
Quotation, not accepted	1-5
Routine acknowledgment	WU
Routine answer to inquiry	WU
General cash book	3-10
General check (canceled)	20-P
Grievance	4 AC
Guarantee/warranty	4 AC

Record	Retention in years
Health safety bulletin	WU-P
Health record (employee)	30 AT or AC
Household move	3 AC
Incorporation record	P
Injury frequency record	10-P
Inspection record	15
Insurance record:	
Expired policy	3-10 AC
Employee	10-P
Property	10 AC
Invention assignment	P
Inventory:	
Plant and equipment	50-P
Supplies	C + 1
Invoice, received, paid	3
Job description	5-8 AC
Labor cost record	3
Law record: federal, state, local	WU
Lawsuit/claim	6 AC-P
Lease record (plant and equipment)	3-6 AC
Letter:	
Descriptive, non-policy-making	1-5
Routine	2-5
License (federal, state, local)	6 AC-P
License agreement and negotiations	20-P
Litigation file	20-P
Maintenance report:	
Building	10 AC
Machinery	5 AC
Record of sold products	10-P
Marketing records:	
Report	WU-10
Research	WU-10
Survey	WU-10
Survey considered historical	P
Mailing list (including bulk, received)	WU
Medical history of employee	30 AT or AC

Record	Retention in years
Medical record:	
Standard	10-30 AV
Minors	to age of majority + 2-6
OSHA	10-30 AV
Mental Health	10-30 AV
Unusual treatment	10-75 AV
Mergers	6 AC-P
Minutes (of board meetings)	P
Mortgage	5 AC
Negative/plate (printing)	CD-10
News ad promotional document	DC-10
Note of appreciation	WU
Notice:	
Of holiday	WU
Of meeting	WU-1
Of transfer	WU
Note register	P
Nuclear production record:	10 AC
Clearance log	25
Cost of service report	25
Life of mortality study data for depreciation purposes	10-25 AC
Normal plant operation	6-10 AC
Procurement record	6
Record of changes to plant	10 AC
Station and system generation	25
Organizational chart	50-P
Patent	15-P
Payroll register (gross/net)	P
Pension record	P
Performance evaluation	5 AT
Petty cash record	3
Planning summary	2
Plant protection record	3-4
Postal record:	
Irregularity	3 AC
Meter record	1

Record	Retention in years
Registered and insured log	1
Price list	1-3
Printing order	2 AC
Production order	2-6 AC
Production record	1-6 AC
Work status report	1-3
Profit and loss statement	P
Publication, bulletin, master	50-P
Public relations record:	
Advertising activity report	5
Community affairs record	P
Contract for advertising	3
Employee activity/promotion	P
Exhibit, release, handout	2-4
In-house promotion	MD-10
Internal publication	P
Layout	1
Manuscript	1
Master	50-P
Photo	1-P
Public information activity	7
Research presentation	P
Tear sheet	2
Purchase order:	
Capital equipment	10 AC
Supplies	3 AC
Quality control report	20-P
Quotation	C + 3
Rate, tariff	WU
Receipt (express registered)	1
Receiving document	2-6 AC
Records management file	6 AC-P
Reliability record	20-P
Report, general	1-P
Retirement record, general	P
Employee's retirement record after employee's death	6

Record	Retention in years
Routing record/transportation	1
Routine acknowledgment (letters and answers)	WU
Safety committee meeting/report	3-4
Safety investigation report	6 AC-P
Salary rates/change	2 AT
Sales order manifest	4
Sales: Analysis/report	5
Contract	3-10 AC
Invoice	3-10 AC
Journal, register	3-15 AC
Order	15 AC-P
Salesforce: Activity report	WU
Commission report	3
Savings report (stock/bonds)	2-3
Seal	6 AC-P
Security: Briefing	3 AT
Violation	50-P
Security bond	3-15 AC
Securities and Exchange Commission report	P
Shipping document (misc.)	2-6
Space allocation	1
Specifications (parts, lists)	20-P
Stock/bond:	
Application	P
Canceled	15
Ledger, transfer, etc.	P
Option	3-10 AC
Stockholders minutes, proxy, etc.	P
Stock savings plan (employees)	50-P
Subcontractor clearance	2
Supplier quality data	15
Taxes:	
Bill/statement	P
Depreciation schedule	P
Excise tax record	P
Return	P
Social security tax record	P

Record	Retention in years
State income tax record	P
State property tax record	P
Unemployment tax record	P
Technical manual/instructions	20-P
Telegram, cable	3
Telephone charges summary	1 AA
Telephone directory (master)	CD
Telephone installation record	1 AA
Time payment/promissory note	3-6 AC
Title paper/tracer report	P
Tool and die design record	20-P
Trade clearance	3 AC
Trademark record	5 AC-P
Traffic inspection report	3-5
Traffic citations	3
Unclaimed wages	C + 2
Union contract	3 AC
Vacation schedule	WU-3
Vehicle record:	
Accident file	2-6 AC
Gas/mileage report	WU
Ledger (cost/expense)	3
Operation/maintenance	2
Transfer/sale	4-6 AC
Vending machine contract	3 AC
Visitor clearance:	
List	2
Log	2-5
Voucher	3
Water rights	10 AC
Work order	1-3
Withholding statement	4-10 AT
X-ray film	7-30
X-ray report:	
In Radiology	2-5 AV
In Medical Record Dept.	10-75 AV

Of course, the above retention guidelines can only be taken as general. They are far from complete. It is recommended that individual regulations be checked out. The federal government requires individuals, corporations, and organizations to keep only four years of records. A number of corporate and other publications recommend different retention periods for the same type of record.[2] It should also be noted that retention periods have yet to be established for microfilm and magnetic data like diskettes and disk packs.

ESTABLISHMENT OF A RETENTION POLICY

In 1980, there was a total of over 1,300 federal statutes and regulations concerning retention of documents.[3] Nonetheless, many applications will be difficult to fit into any retention guideline. In such cases it is up to the records manager and the organization management to develop appropriate retention policies. Also, in cases when the records manager disagrees with retention practice, the establishment of a retention period is necessary. Five criteria should enter this decision-making process: (1) file station demand and users' requirements; (2) potential demand within the organization other than regular users' requirements; (3) legal, obligatory, and related guidelines; (4) archival values; and (5) economic considerations.[4] The objectives in such a decision-making process are to ensure that (1) documents that must be maintained in accordance with applicable laws and regulations are preserved for as long as necessary; (2) documents necessary for the conduct of business are filed in a systematic manner and are accessible when necessary; (3) documents relevant to foreseeable or pending judicial, administrative, or congressional investigations or proceedings are identified and preserved; (4) documents that must be maintained on a long-term or permanent basis are catalogued and stored according to long-term storage requirements; and (5) all other documents are destroyed.[5]

In discussions about the design of a retention policy the key word *statutes* comes up regularly. Many of the 50 states have developed statutes of limitations, which specify the time after which legal rights cannot be enforced by civil action in court. This means that once a record reaches the age beyond which the statute of limitation applies, the record is valueless as evidence in a court of law. It must be noted that the statute of limitations *does not* require record keeping. It simply says that no action can be brought against you, nor can you initiate an action against someone else, after a period of a certain number of years.[6]

The most common belief is that records, particularly business records, should be kept for seven years. The idea of keeping records for seven years probably derives from English common law, which picked it up from the Bible: "At the end of every seven years you shall grant a release" (Deuteronomy 15:1).[7]

In order to establish a retention schedule, a record retention comittee should be formed to set the value of the records to the organization or company. First, the volume of each record system must be established. The next step is to examine the file's contents in light of the five criteria listed above. The committee should draft a proposed retention policy to be submitted to management or corporate decision makers.

One of the key areas in this process is the investigation of duplicate records, that is, records kept in duplicate for the functional requirements of a department. Only the original record is required for legal reasons; the duplicate should be kept only as long as functional requirements demand. A typical example is the medical record in clinics and hospitals. There is no legal need for the radiology department, the laboratory, or any other department to keep records of patients' treatments as long as the same information is stored in the medical record in the medical records department.

A retention policy, once management and all concerned personnel have agreed to it, has the following advantages: (1) it eliminates the onerous expense of storing irrelevant and obsolete documents; (2) it reduces the burden and cost of document retrieval in response to functional requests, government investigation, or litigation; (3) it reduces substantially the legal risk flowing from documents, particularly those which are hastily drafted, erroneous, or misleading; and (4) it averts adverse interference from the nonproduction of documents in litigation.[8]

We should also keep in mind, however, the disadvantages of a retention policy and its implementation: (1) the expense of establishing and administering a program including the commitment of human and capital resources needed to assure compliance; (2) the inability to prove a fact definitely because documents have been destroyed; (3) a diminished flexibility of response to formal and informal requests for documents; (4) adverse inferences arising from selective destruction outside the boundaries of the program (destroying documents appears less corrupt in the absence of a program or policy); and (5) other adverse legal and public relation effects, including the discoverability of the program.[9]

Experience has shown that a retention policy is particularly needed when the records department is running out of space. Considerations of alternatives to space shortage usually list a carefully planned retention policy first.

SPACE PLANNING

Once the volume and retention period are established, space planning can be considered. In most cases the records department is either running out or short of space. It is imperative that space be planned wisely and used in the most economical way possible. When analyzing space availability for record storage we have to include all record rooms, satellite file rooms, and any off-site space. If files are overcrowded and there is no additional space available, then different equipment or systems may be required. But even when sufficient space is available, it should be used very economically. Space is very expensive, and space costs are a substantial part of record storage costs, as will be shown.

For planning purposes, all available space must be listed. It is helpful to do a simple drawing of the file area(s). An architect's plan is the best aid in planning space and layout of a record storage system. If an architect's plan is not available, it is worth the effort to take a tape and measure the rooms, making note of doors, support columns, and other features. Lighting is important as well and should be indicated on each drawing.

If there is the possibility of a need for high-density storage equipment, then check the floor loading capacity of each individual storage room well in advance. This capacity should be stated in pounds per square foot, live load, or kilograms per square meter, live load.[10]

Also, since cost of space varies greatly with location, it is worthwhile to establish the annual cost of space per square foot (or square meter) in your area. If storage is facilitated in different buildings, the cost of space should be established for each individual storage room or building. For instance, an office record area has a different space cost than an off-site storage record center. Obviously, space in Manhattan is much more costly than in a small town in Nebraska, and different space costs make it reasonable to select different equipment for each location. The cost of occupying one square foot of space per year at 1982 values in Boston is $16-18; Manhattan, $22-29; and Los Angeles, $17-21. The national average is $12.

Some filing equipment is more space-efficient than others. Space efficiency factors will provide a general guide for how much space is required for a certain volume.

FILING AND ACTIVITY

In view of the increase in costs for record keeping, a question arises as to the value of keeping old records. The record system is the memory of an organization, an essential element in any organization's functioning. The key to a smooth-running organization is its filing system, and the key to planning a smooth-running filing system is an evaluation of space and activity. While we cannot overlook the space requirements, activity is a factor which is more difficult to establish. There is some information in record systems that is (almost) never retrieved, but it has to be kept for policy or legal reasons on a long-term basis; other information might be drawn upon every day. Most records fit into one of three categories of activity: periodic, random, or active.

Periodic activity refers to an application in which after a short period of time during which there are frequent requests there is almost no activity.

Records of telephone calls kept in telephone companies would be typical of this kind of application. Who wants to know what calls were made after six months or one year? Inquiries requiring records of when and whom you called would be made at the time of billing or shortly thereafter.

Random activity indicates a lack of pattern in the time and number of requests from the filing system. A typical application would be sales records of specialized, made-to-order items. The customer may buy another piece a few weeks or years later. In this case the record has to provide product data, costs, and price. The record is vital for the next estimate and sale, but no one can foresee when the customer will want another item. Another example of this kind of activity may be personnel records for active employees. Apart from the regular activities, like performance evaluations, one never knows when the record will be requested.

The third category is *case activity*. As long as a case is open, information on that case will be required and must be readily available. Many records in law offices fall into this category, as do the medical records of clinics and hospitals. Although one never knows when a person will require treatment in a hospital, 80 percent of all requests for information have to do with patients who are treated for a medical problem, which constitutes a case. Records of large buildings, most architects' files, and records of case histories are typical of this category. The status of activity can be determined by considering the space available for active filing and the expected time period of activity. For instance, a lawyer's case file may be active until a settlement is reached, but if the settlement is to be monitored or adjusted on a regular basis, then the record should stay in the active file. In a hospital or clinic the medical record should be kept active for at least three months, or six months after the last visit or discharge date.

Once a record loses its active status, it should be purged and moved into the semiactive file. For instance, in a hospital the semiactive file contains all the records the hospital can keep in that record room. For semiactive records, equipment of higher density and less accessibility can be selected. The index would show the date of the last visit and/or discharge date, and one could determine from this information which time span has passed since the last visit or discharge and thus which file holds the record.

Any record that should be kept longer than the actual space in the file room allows should be moved into the inactive file. An inactive file could be located in a room in the basement, an off-site storage facility, or on microfilm. In medical applications, for instance, the inactive file should have less than 10 percent of the total activity of the record system but may represent 70-90 percent of the total volume. The active file may have 10-15 percent of the volume but more than 80 percent of the activity. These figures vary, of course, by application. Each of these three categories requires a different organization and structure for the filing system. Different criteria should be used when selecting equipment.

SELECTING EQUIPMENT BY ACTIVITY

For periodic activity, the period of activity should be established for each application and then the records should be divided into active and inactive categories. Active records are kept in a special file that is very accessible and close to requesting areas. Such active records could be stored in conventional cabinets, on lateral shelves, in work station equipment, on microfilm, or on line on computer. Of course, active records should not be stored in mobile shelving systems with insufficient aisle space, off site, or in any less accessible equipment or location. For inactive records, any high-density storage system with low cost factors will do.

For random activity, all records are to be kept equally accessible. Power files, mobile shelving with sufficient aisles, of Times Two-type equipment is recommended. The individual selection is, of course, guided by the nature of each application and the volume of the record system. When binders are used and they fill up to maximum capacity, for instance, a second binder can be stored right next to the original one, identified by an additional number or letter.

Case activity requires different systems for each level of activity and equipment chosen accordingly. For case activity applications, we differentiate among active, semiactive, and inactive filing. While the case is active, the record should be kept in an active file consisting of equipment of maximum accessibility. For instance, stationary shelving could be used as long as sufficient aisle space is provided for multiple simultaneous access. The active file should be close to work stations or desks in order to shorten walking distance to a minimum and reduce search time. The semiactive file can be the storage system in the main file room next to the main office. These records should not represent more than 20 percent of the activity, whereas the active file may have as much as 85 percent of the total activity. The inactive file would hold records that have to be kept for legal or research reasons, and the activity level there might be 10 percent or less. These records should be stored in the most economical equipment or system available, be it high-density storage equipment, off-site storage, or microfilm. When planning a record system, the records manager should analyze activity levels carefully. This can be done by a survey recording all records being pulled by age and linking them to the last activity. Filing by activity requires sufficient data on activity levels for records. These data enable the records manager to select space and filing equipment accordingly. It can be disastrous to use just volume and space as decision-influencing factors in the selection of equipment and can lead to millions of dollars being wasted in equipment, especially mobile shelving systems, which are often purchased with no consideration for activity and accessibility. Many systems had to be taken out after a short time as a result. Understanding the relationship among records, space, and activity is the key to a smooth-running information storage system.

NOTES

1. See the space efficiency list in Chapter 3.

2. See *Record Retention Schedule: A Fast Guide to Record Retention* (Newark: New Jersey Society of Certified Public Accountants, August 1967); J. O. Aspley, *Specific Record Groups*, Office Administration Handbook (Chicago: Dartnell Corp., 1975); W. A. Hancock, ed., *"Record Retention Guide,"* The Lawyer's Brief 7, no. 25 (December 12, 1977); Harry Huffman, Doland J. Mulkerne, and Allien Russon, *Records Retention, Office Procedures and Administration* (New York: McGraw-Hill, 1965); Phyllis M. Lybarger, *Records Retention Scheduling* (Prairie Village, Kan.: Association of Records Managers and Administrators, 1980); Michigan Department of Management and Budget, Office Services Division, *Records Disposal: General Schedule No. 2*, Administrative manual (1977); William E. Mitchell, *Recommended Schedule: Records Retention*, 10th ed. (Evansville, Ind.: Ellsworth, 1976); *Records Retention Schedule for 600 Common Business Papers: Retention and Preservation of Records with Destructive Schedules*, 9th ed. (Chicago: Records Controls, 1977); *Suggested Retention Schedule for Business Records: Records Control and Storage Handbook with Retention Schedules* (Franklin Park, Ill.: Bankers Box Records Storage Systems, 1977); *Retention of Accounting Records* (San Jose: California Moving and Storage Association, 1977); Robert A. Shiff, *Normal Records, Records Retention: Normal and Disaster*, Pt. 1 (Washington, D.C.: Small Business Administration, 1970); Olive R. Surgen, *Schedules of Records and Periods of Retention, Records Management Fundamentals* (West Hyattsville, Md.: Information and Business Systems, 1973); General Services Administration, National Archives and Record Service, *General Record Schedules* (Washington, D.C.: Government Printing Office, 1977); Bertha M. Weeks, "Tabulation of Over 300 Common Papers Found in a Normal Business Office with Lengths of Time Retained," *Filing and Records Management*, 3d ed. (New York: Ronald Press, 1964).

3. Ibid.

4. John M. Fedders and Lauryn H. Guttenplan, "Document Retention and Destruction: Practical, Legal and Ethical Considerations," *Notre Dame Lawyer* 56, no. 1 (October 1980).

5. Thomas Wilds, *Records Retention and Files Management: Seminar Workbook* (New York: Thomas Wilds Associates, 1980).

6. Fedders and Guttenplan, "Document Retention and Destruction."

7. Lybarger, *Records Retention Scheduling*, p. 26.

8. Ibid.

9. Ibid.

10. Live load is in contrast to actual load. Live load means that the weight of the object is to be spread over an area rather than concentrated at a point.

2

EQUIPMENT EVALUATION

DRAWER CABINETS

The most common kind of filing equipment is the four-drawer cabinet. It is usually the type of filing system one starts out with and everyone knows how to deal with it. Folders and binders are usually indexed at the top, and filing often means simply dropping documents into the right container. Comparatively, however, this filing equipment uses more space than any other kind. Having to pull out the drawer for accessibility slows down the filing operation. To increase capacity and offset some of the space wasting, cabinets with five drawers may be used. Suspended pockets, although more expensive and more space consuming, improve neatness and provide better guidance.

LATERAL FILES

The category of lateral files covers a wide range of equipment. In every case the documents are arranged like books on book shelves, the side edge facing the person looking at them. For large filing systems, open shelving is the most economical and efficient equipment. There are three types of open shelving equipment. First, individual tiers can be arranged into shelving sections. They offer the advantage of easy assembly and rearrangement (see Plate 2.1). Second, cantilever shelving, also called center-style shelving, is constructed of a center upright with shelves hanging out like branches of a tree. Optional end panels give this type of shelving an attractive office appeal. Last, industrial shelving is the most common kind used for economical storage applications: usually four uprights holding shelves that are connected to the uprights.

2.1   Lateral file consisting of individual tiers. ThinLine® Conserv-a-
file® . Courtesy of Supreme Equipment and Systems Corporation.

As mentioned before, lateral files are space saving compared with drawer
files. Open shelving is certainly more cost efficient than drawer cabinets,
but it does not satisfy every application's security or indexing needs. In
large installations where a record room can be locked, open shelving may be
acceptable. When records require some security measures and are kept in a
general office, open shelving cannot be used. For office file security the
filing industry is providing a range of closed lateral cabinets (see Plate 2.2).

Files with pullouts have panels and are enclosed. Each individual shelf
has a pullout mechanism. This makes the folders and their index more
accessible. Files with pullouts are a compromise between drawer files and
shelf files. The pullout mechanism requires a wider aisle between the files
and therefore more space (see Plate 2.3).

Closed cabinet shelf files are enclosed lateral files. They are used in
offices where security of records is required. Individual shelves each have
their own door. They require less space than pullout files and provide the

2.2   Lateral cabinet. Courtesy Supreme Equipment and Systems Corporation.

security of enclosed file cabinets while having a low space-efficiency factor, that is, they use less space than equipment with higher space-efficiency factors.

A data box file or a data box shelving unit is a lateral file or shelving unit with plastic or metal boxes either hanging from rails or standing on shelves. The boxes are usually four inches wide and provide for neat appearance of the system. Each box can be individually labeled. It should be noted, however, that these boxes are using up valuable additional space (see Plate 2.4).

Lateral filing always requires a sufficient number of shelf dividers, except those units with data boxes. The dividers keep folders and binders in upright position. At least two dividers are required per shelf, except with terminal digital filing, which usually requires three or four dividers per shelf.

Having compared conventional drawer filing with lateral filing, we can now look at mechanical filing devices. Automated and high-density storage equipment are designed to use space more efficiently. Some products also make filing systems more efficient in regard to retrieval time and file control and even save personnel. As the term indicates, high-density filing equipment stores files in greater density and increases storage capacity in a given space. These systems are mechanical, with or without a motor drive, and some are designed as work station systems. In work station systems the

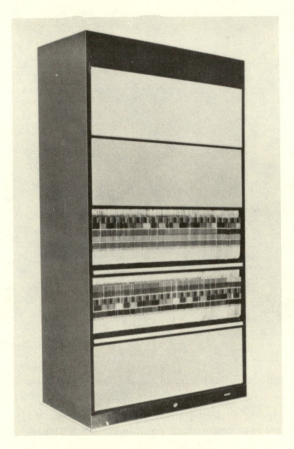

2.3   Lateral cabinet with retractable doors. Courtesy
Datafile Ltd.

equipment brings the records to the operator rather than a file clerk having to search physically for the record. High-density equipment can be divided into three types: rotary equipment, work station systems, and movable or sliding equipment.

ROTARY SYSTEMS

There is a range or rotary files available, most of them for card filing applications. The classical circular file has a central upright. Five round tiers circulate around this central shaft. This makes the circular file very accessible. Its space efficiency is remarkable, although not as remarkable as its sellers claim. The problem is whether one uses the inner or the outer circumference to compute capacity. The promoters of the circular file claim that most records are more bulky on one side due to paper clips,

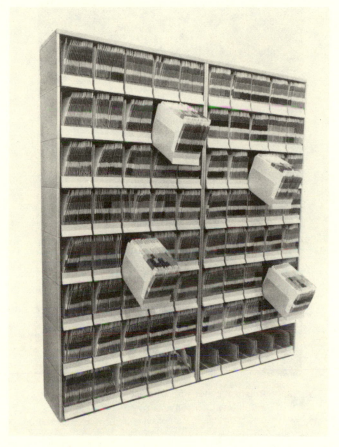

2.4   Lateral shelving with box-type sections. Courtesy Supreme
Equipment and Systems Corp.

staples, and other similar items, and as a result space is wasted in a linear
file. This is partly true, but the increase in bulk due to these items may be
minimal or nonexistent, depending on the record application and the paper
procedures. For instance, Mr. Gillotte, producer of Gyroblique, claims that
the capacity of this circular file is more than the outer circumference.[1] The
fact is that the capacity is less than the outer circumference. Depending on
how many staples, paper clips, and so forth used, the capacity is somewhere
between the linear capacity of the inner circumference and the outer circumference of the circular file. For purposes of comparison, the author has used
a 50 percent usage in the space-efficiency listing.[2]

The best-known kind of rotating equipment is the power file, a motorized
file unit in which carriers rotate horizontally. Available since the 1950s, it
was called the automated file of the 1960s and early 1970s (see Plates 2.5-6).
These units are available from companies like Kardex Systems, Inc., of

2.5   Rotary file unit with five tiers. Courtesy Robert
P. Gillotte Company.

Marietta, Ohio (formerly Remington Rand), Acme Visible Records, Inc., of
Crozet, Virginia, the White Corporation of New Jersey (manufacturing and
marketing the former Diebold Powerfiles), and LeFebure of Grand Rapids,
Iowa (selling the Simplawheel, mainly to the banking market). These units
make maximum use of room height and eliminate stretching and bending.
The operator sits in front of the unit, using a posting board as a work area,
and a true file-work station is created. Such units are available in various
heights, that is, with 14, 16, 18, and 20 carriers.

Kardex Systems, of Marietta, Ohio, markets its Lektriever Series 80, an
"automated storage and retrieval system with computer interface capability." Using a microprocessor, the system monitors location and status of
each record. Cross-reference capabilities are helpful because the system
provides security and/or can provide its own index reference. By keying in
the record number, the system will identify the location of the record,
activate the Lektriever, and automatically make the appropriate carrier
arrive at the posting board. In addition, the readout will show the operator
the location of the record. Here is one of the rare cases when filing com-

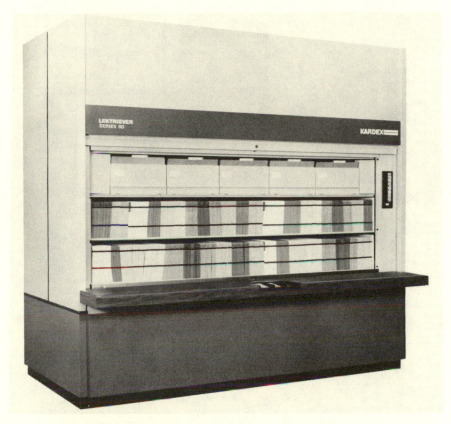

2.6   Lektriever™, the well-known automated filing unit from Kardex, formerly Remington Rand. Courtesy Kardex Systems, Inc.

panies have interfaced mechanical filing devices with computer technology in order to manage hard copy.

A less sophisticated system is Times Two, a cabinet with double-faced shelving that can be rotated to make both sides of the shelving accessible (see Plate 2.7). The Times Two system eliminates the need for a second aisle, and this makes it space saving. Being enclosed and lockable, it provides for a neat record cabinet that is not dependent on any power service but provides the advantages of a mechanical system. It is also flexible enough for use in an active system. Acme Visible Records, Inc., markets a competitive unit under the name Rotomatic.

A unique system is available from the White Power Files Corporation. It is called No-Walk and, as the name indicates, is designed to eliminate walking in the file room. No-Walk is a combination of a rotating system

2.7 Rotating double-sided cabinet. Rotomatic®. Courtesy Acme Visible Records, Inc.

2.8 No-Walk. Individual file sections rotate on a track and chain system. Courtesy White Power Files, Inc.

and a work station system (see Plate 2.8). Individual short shelving sections travel on circular tracks and are pulled by a chain until the desired section stops in front of the work station. By touching the controls the file clerk can order the file section to be worked on. The same technology is known to work at "cleaners" and in coat rooms, whose racks are actually manufactured by the same company.

WORK STATION SYSTEMS

Other work station systems do not rotate but bring a container with records to the operator. Records are filed in steel boxes that are stacked on both sides of the center aisle. This aisle is narrow, as only a column is moving vertically and horizontally in it. This device pulls the desired box out of the stack and delivers it to the operator. Such systems are available from Supreme Equipment and Systems Corporation (Minitrieve) and Access Corporation (System M) (see Plate 2.9). Supreme Equipment and Systems Corporation of Brooklyn, New York, also developed a record trace system for its Minitrieve system. The Minitrieve is a unique type of automated filing equipment: It provides a work station to which the machine brings the records. Particularly well suited for medium activity and work station requirements, it can save floor space, as the space-efficiency factors for most Minitrieve configurations are in the .40-.30 range. Special security is provided. Supreme claims an average cycle time of 27 seconds for its

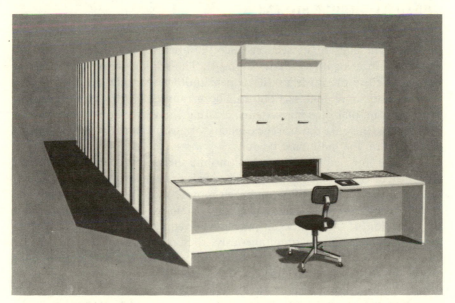

2.9   Workstation Minitrieve® . Courtesy Supreme Equipment and Systems Corp.

smallest unit. Users have been reporting that the equipment raises employees' morale because it "promotes" file clerks to equipment operators.

Access Corporation of Cincinnati, Ohio, has its System M combined with an individual search and select device that searches and selects the individual card or wallet. Actually, the system will make the document pop up. The operator has only to retrieve the clearly marked record. Unfortunately, this system is only available for card, wallet and microfilm systems. It is mainly used for microfiche, microfilm jackets, and microfilm documents like aperture cards, but it can also be used for eight-by-five cards or wallets.

LATERAL MOBILE SHELVING

The most effective mechanical type of high-density storage is mobile shelving, of which there are two kinds. With one system, lateral mobile shelving, the shelving faces the person standing in front of it with its full width (see Plate 2.10). A second row (or third for Tri-file) of shelving is positioned right behind it (see Plate 2.11). To access the back row you move the shelving in front to its left or right. The system does not require any motors or mechanical aid, which is a great advantage. However, users dislike the lack of a handle. Existing shelving can be used, but care must be taken that no uprights with sharp edges are used at the operator's front due to the risk of cutting a hand. This kind of mobile shelving is available from Supreme, Thinline, Tennsco, and other vendors (see Manufacturers Index).

VERTICAL MOBILE SHELVING

The second and most common kind of mobile shelving is vertical mobile shelving. The ends of its sections face the operator standing (outside the system) in front of it (see Plates 2.12-14). The sections move to the left or right and close one aisle as they open another. Mobile shelving is very flexible, and individual sections can be arranged as the layout requires. With most mobile shelving systems, existing shelving can be used. Mobile shelving can increase the storage capacity of any given room 60-90 percent, depending on the individual layout.

However, for two reasons vertical mobile shelving is often disliked. One is the lack of accessibility. If mobile shelving is designed with no consideration for activity and accessibility (and each mobile shelving unit is individually designed and assembled in modules), the system may not be acceptable to a file operation. If the number of people who require access to such a system cannot enter the system simultaneously, they may have to line up outside the system waiting for the system to become accessible. Such waiting lines can be annoying, but they also could cripple a file operation. The records manager has to decide how much accessibility is required for the file operation and on that basis determines the number of aisles required.

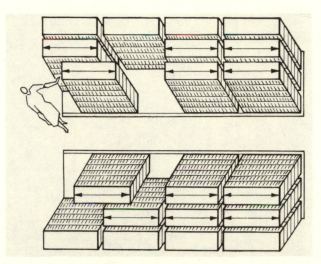

2.10 Lateral mobile shelving. Files in rear row are stationary, while those in front and middle rows roll to either side, at fingertip touch, to give access to all rows. Roll-Away ThinLine Tri-file® systems. Courtesy Supreme Equipment and Systems Corp.

2.11 Lateral mobile shelving. Here only one tier is moved for accessibility. Courtesy Supreme Equipment and Systems Corp.

2.12   Vertical mobile shelving, motorized version. Courtesy Acme Visible Records, Inc.

Sales representatives of companies that sell mobile shelving are usually not trained to assess ongoing activity or to make recommendations in regard to the number of aisles required. If a records manager does not know the activity of a filing section, a survey can easily be done by observing how many persons work simultaneously during peak hours in the area to be converted to mobile shelving and multiplying this number by the factor representing the increase of volume. The present system would be factor 1.0, and any increase in capacity is to be added (i.e., a 50 percent increase = a factor of 1.5). For instance, if at present three people work simultaneously during peak hours at the files positioned where the new mobile shelving system will be installed and the proposal shows an increase of 80 percent storage capacity, then between five and six aisles (3 × 1.8 = 5.4) are required for this system.

The second disadvantage is that mobile shelving can be heavy and difficult to move. One inch of paper (letter-size) weighs between 1.8 and 2.5 pounds. This means that the payload for a three-foot-wide, seven-tier shelving unit, letter-size, is just over 1,000 pounds. A three-foot-wide, five-tier X-ray film storage unit would weigh almost 4,000 pounds! When you multiply this weight by the number of three-foot sections planned in your mobile shelving unit, you may come up with a very heavy load. Do you have to employ only strong file clerks with body building experience capable of

2.13   Vertical mobile shelving, mechanical assisted version. Courtesy
White Power Files, Inc.

moving thousands of pounds constantly? Of course not, if you plan your
system carefully and select the appropriate equipment and layout.

In planning a mobile shelving system, it is important to consider the
following factors: (1) layout; (2) weight to be moved; (3) how sections are
going to be moved (motorized, mechanical assist, or direct manpower); (4)
the safety system planned; and (5) how many aisles are required.

Regarding the layout, for better access and maintenance it is preferable to
have a center aisle with two units on each side rather than one big unit with
an aisle close to the wall.

A center aisle may waste 7-15 percent of the space, but it is very
advantageous with respect to accessibility and maintenance. A unit with a
center aisle can usually be moved by hand and does not require motoriza-
tion or safety devices. Also, if a problem develops with one section, the

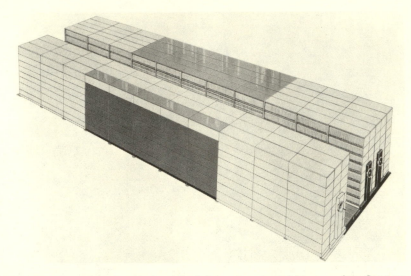

2.14   Configuration of vertical mobile shelving: its potential for expansion. Courtesy
Supreme Equipment and Systems Corp.

other side is still operable. And since sections are shorter and carry less
weight, they require only a manual or nonmotorized unit, which is substantially lower in cost.

There are a dozen or so companies manufacturing mobile shelving. What
guidelines could be used for selecting equipment? First, if a manual system
is planned, one has to examine ease of movement. Every company claims
that its system is easier to move than the competition's and for various
reasons. Some vendors of mobile shelving even provide figures of how
many pounds of pressure are necessary to move a thousand pounds or a
multiple thereof. Because there are no national standards on the procedure
of collecting such data, though, one has to be very careful with these data.

It is quite confusing to listen to sales arguments when selecting mobile
shelving and the "best" vendor. Different technical reasons are usually
given as to why company A's product is better than company B's. What is a
good way to find out what is valid or what is true?

Personally, I recommend a system with mechanical assistance. Mechanical assistance means that there is a chain drive connected to a wheel or
sprocket system. Such devices are based on the technology of the ten-speed
bicycle. In order to achieve the same movement you turn the wheel (instead
of the pedal on a bike) either for one cycle with more pressure or for more
cycles with less pressure per cycle. The gear ratio for only one cycle uses
much more power. If you choose the gear ratio for multiple cycles, you'll
find that you can move the wheel at your shelving section much easier. Of
course, the difference between a bicycle and mobile shelving unit is that
with a bicycle you can change gears, whereas with the mobile shelving unit

you select the gear in advance, that is, when you buy it. Different companies offer different gear ratios. Mechanical assistance is dependent on the ratio of sprockets used between the drive shaft in the carrier and the operating wheel. Records managers should question prospective vendors of mobile shelving about their ratio in the sprocket system. It has been my experience that sales arguments claiming "easier movement" because of "better drive mechanism," "bigger drive wheels," "less resistance on the tracks," and so on should be examined very critically and may turn out to be mere sales rhetoric.

Certain occasions do call for a motorized mobile shelving unit, and it certainly eliminates all worries of moving tons of weight all day. At the touch of a button, a row or group of sections moves to open the desired aisle. Motorized units are more expensive than manual or mechanically assisted units, and the price difference is due to not only the motor. Actually, in themselves the small electrical motors used do not change the cost of a mobile shelving unit much. The difference is usually in the safety system. Manual and mechanically assisted mobile shelving units generally do not require specific safety measures. If a section moves while a person is in the system, he or she can push the section back. However, when a motor or a number of individual motors are involved, the possibility of someone getting hurt is great. Therefore, all motorized mobile shelving systems require a safety system. Three safety systems are available, and a records manager can choose one or a combination of two or three safety systems, if required.

The system involving the lowest costs is the dead man switch. A button or lever attached to the front panel controls each section. The button activates the motor, which moves the section. When the operator stops pressing the button or lever, the section stops. This device necessitates that the operator literally walk along with the moving section. While walking with a section to close an aisle, the operator is expected to check this aisle first to see that no one and nothing is inside the system or inside the aisle. If a person or object is in the aisle, the operator can release the button or lever, deactivating the drive system and causing the moving section to stop instantly.

This dead man safety switch is often installed in motorized mobile shelving systems when no particular safety system is specified in the bid, quotation, or purchase order. It has the lowest cost of all safety systems. But file clerks often dislike it because it tempts others with access to the unit to play games like "let's squeeze him a little" and "let's scare her for a second."

Safety bars are the second kind of safety system available for motorized mobile shelving. Safety bars are contact lines or bars at foot or hip height with an additional bar at shoulder height. The bars are attached to the shelving along individual sections and run parallel to the shelves within each aisle. When they come in contact with an object or person, they deactivate the system and the unit stops instantly.

Should someone be in the aisle when the system starts to move, touching one of the safety bars will stop the moving section immediately. However, there have been cases when file clerks were concentrating on their work when the system started suddenly moving toward them. They got so frightened when the "whole wall of shelving" approached that they "froze." Although they screamed, they could not move to touch one of the contact bars. When the system finally touched them, without hurting them physically, of course, the section stopped but the file clerks had to be hospitalized for shock treatment.

The third kind of safety system for motorized mobile shelving is the safety floor, which uses the same technology as automated doors. Sensors in the ground are activated when weight is put on the floor, that is, when someone steps on it, and they shut off the power. Thus the weight of a person standing in an aisle will shut off the power of that mobile shelving unit.

Safety floor is the most expensive, but also the best-liked safety system in mobile shelving. It too has its catches, however. For instance, when people are standing on the tracks within an aisle, the sensors are to be activated and there is no guard against accidents unless the person literally takes a step (into the sensor zone) when someone tries to close that aisle. Also, short file clerks tend to step on the bottom shelf in order to reach the top shelf. Again, in this case there is no safety guard against accidents. Also, it is worthwhile to find out what the minimum weight limit is for activating the sensors. Accidents have been reported from users who left a stool, file cart, or lightweight object in the aisle. The sensors in the floor were not activated because the weight of the object was under the minimum limit. The object was sometimes jammed, sometimes crushed, and in some cases there was damage to the shelving and the total system.

The best precaution against accidents is a combination of safety floor and safety bars. It is important that the safety bars be well positioned and the safety floor well tuned. In speaking to more than a thousand mobile shelving users in the United States, Europe, and other parts of the world, I have never heard of a major accident involving mobile shelving in which anyone got seriously hurt. Manufacturers of mobile shelving use motors of little impact, usually a quarter horsepower or less. I have seen contests between sales representatives who activated the system and then stood in the aisle, competing to see how many activated sections they could hold back. Even when people got literally squeezed in, the worst physical damage I have heard of are bruises. The safety question is admittedly more psychological, but it is an important one. If file clerks working with a system do not feel safe, they will hesitate to use the system, which will cause inefficiencies in the filing department.

As with power files, there have been attempts to link motorized vertical mobile shelving with computers. Individual companies have been designing and installing systems with links to computers. The motorized vertical mobile shelving system can be activated or deactivated by a microprocessor, which will indicate to the operator in which section the record can be found (if it is not charged out). The system itself will open the right aisle before the file clerk gets there, and in some cases a light indicates where the record can be found, that is, on which side and shelf. Such computer capabilities can be linked to the safety system. When someone is retrieving or inserting a record, the system will not be mechanically operable and will indicate to anyone who wants to move the sections that to do so may be dangerous.

Vertical mobile shelving systems are the most commonly used sort of high-density storage equipment. However, before planning the purchase of such a system, the records manager has to make sure the designated area in a building will take the weight of a high-density storage system. The fact that almost double the volume of a conventional shelving system can be stored in a high-density storage system means that there may be as much as twice the weight on the floor. Users report that floors have been giving in and ceilings crack under the sheer weight of mobile shelving units once fully loaded. Strengthening the floor can be troublesome and very costly. Therefore, it is advisable to check well ahead of the purchase the weight capacity of the designated area for mobile shelving. Floor loading capacity is expressed in pounds per square foot, live load, or in kilograms per square meter, live load. In order to compare the expected weight of the loaded system with the floor loading capacity we have to establish the expected weight of the system when fully loaded. The weight of the system consists of two factors. The first is the net weight of the mobile shelving system itself when unloaded, including the floor, tracking, carriages, shelving, and all accessories. This weight should be obtained from the prospective vendor. Second is the payload of the system, which usually cannot be obtained from a prospective vendor as it depends on the individual application, namely, the weight of the documents stored, their density, and the arrangement.

The best way to establish the weight of records stored is to take a typical section of your files and weigh the records. Let us assume that you find a typical shelf of your records 36 inches long. Take these records, weigh them, and divide the weight by 36 to compute the weight per filing inch. For instance, if all records taken off a 36-inch-wide shelf weigh 72 pounds, then the weight per LFI is 2 pounds. If there are various types of density and materials, you would have to weigh representative sections and compute an overall figure. By multiplying the weight per filing inch by the number of filing inches the proposed system will hold, you compute the payload of your mobile shelving system. By adding this to the net weight of the equipment itself, you get the total expected weight of the mobile shelving system when fully loaded.

Here are some guidelines. A filing inch of hard copy paper records weighs between 1.8 and 2.2 pounds per inch, or 40-50 kilograms per linear filing meter. X-ray film jackets filled with standard sized X-ray films, for instance, weigh 8-12 pounds per linear filing inch (standard hospital size). The weights of plans, drawings, and other storage media vary with size and material used.

Once the total expected weight is established, a structural engineer or architect should establish the live floor loading capacity of the designated area. Of course, the records manager should know floor loading capacities for all storage areas because they will be required when equipment is planned or rearranged.

One possible pitfall can arise with any mobile shelving system: the development of a low point. Mobile shelving systems have to be installed carefully, particularly with respect to the floor. Its tracks have to be leveled completely and shimmed properly. All too often this process is not carried out correctly. Then the system develops a low point: because of the tremendous weight the subfloor and/or tracking system tends to bend. The system becomes at one point a little lower than everywhere else. The difference between the required level of the tracking and the low point can be from an eighth of an inch to more than one inch. The heavy filing sections tend to roll toward that low point and, according to the law of physics, tend to stay there. When you want to access the file you have to move the sections away from the low point and then hold them away while you are in the aisle.

Repairing such installations can cause substantial inconvenience. The file has to be unloaded, shelving dismantled, and the floor and tracking repaired. Some companies offer floor systems that can be adjusted later. In any case, a paragraph should be added to the bid or purchase order stating that the vendor has to repair any such low point free of charge, during nonworking hours, including unloading and loading the file.

MICROFILM AND OFF-SITE STORAGE

The most space can be saved by converting to microfilm. There is no doubt that microfilm achieves the most substantial savings of space. Reducing the size of a document to a small photographic image can eliminate most space problems. However, before entering a microfilm program one has to consider a range of topics, including cost compared with hard copy (see Chapter 3); other alternatives; equipment selection; in-house versus service microfilming; and preservation of microfilm for long-term storage (see Chapter 4).

Another tool one should consider when planning and evaluating archival and inactive records is off-site record storage. Sometimes acceptable for semiactive records, but mainly used for inactive or archival records, off-site storage is a real solution to space shortage. It is in a way a competitor to high-density storage equipment and microfilm.

However, off-site storage is not as common as its alternatives. Organizations are often reluctant to store valuable or confidential records outside their premises and are very concerned about security and confidentiality. This reluctance is weakening as more and more organizations get used to the idea of off-site storage and because off-site storage has an excellent track record. I have not heard of any major security or confidentiality problems. If the building used is safe and secure, there should be no problem with off-site storage. The idea of off-site storage is that one takes inactive records with a low retrieval rate and stores them off the premises in a conveniently located low-cost building, thus reducing the cost of occupying space substantially. Low activity should require a low retrieval rate, but even for this low retrieval rate one should organize an appropriate retrieval system.

The low-cost and convenient building for off-site storage could be a barn in the area or a closed down gas station. Any low-cost building that is safe and secure will do. Of course, the closer it is located to the main organization, the better. Commercial off-site storage companies will store your records in industrial buildings, under mountains (in former mines), or in storage facilities, sometimes up to hundred miles away from the record department. The federal government has similar storage centers for its inactive record storage.

There are three ways one can approach the establishment and use of off-site storage. The first is to organize an off-site storage facility for the requirements of a records department. This is possible if the department has enough volume and sufficient financial resources to start its own off-site program for inactive records. Then the records department can rent or purchase a suitable building, and the records manager can arrange for the required equipment, procedures, retrieval arrangements, transportation shuttles, and personnel. Alternatively, if there is not enough volume for the records department to start its own off-site program, the records manager may find additional departments within the same organization prepared for a joint venture. If various departments that require storage space (not necessarily only for records) pool their resources, a joint off-site storage facility could be started. The third way is to find a suitable partner to join in this venture. For instance, hospitals have successfully entered into such joint ventures.

If off-site storage facilities organized by your department are not possible, there is always the commercial off-site storage company. Such enterprises can be found in every part of the country. In fact, it seems to be the fastest growing industry in the record storage field in the late 1970s and early 1980s. Commercial record centers will collect inactive records and store them for you. When you require information from records stored in their storage centers, they will retrieve the record and ship it to you as quickly as possible. Retrieval times and charges depend on distances to offices, established retrieval schedules, and transportation schedules. Most storage centers guarantee safe and secure storage combined with confidentiality in handling. For emergency service, there should be an electronic transcribing machine, particularly if the distance between the record department and the off-site facility is more than five miles and records may be needed on an emergency basis. Again, a commercial storage facility should be checked out for its experience and competency. The National Association of Record Storage Centers, located in Minneapolis, may be of help in this selection.

It is worthwhile to check retrieval levels regularly in order to avoid storage of relatively active records in the off-site facility. I cannot stress enough that only inactive records should be stored in such a facility. Remember, filing systems with random activity are usually not suited for off-site storage. For cost comparison, refer to Chapter 3 on cost management.

DOCUMENT CONTAINERS

There have been very few changes in the field of document containers over the last hundred years. Almost the exact same styles of file folders, document wallets, and data boxes could have been found in the late nineteenth century as today. Actually, the main difference is the stock from which containers are made, and the way folders are arranged. In the United States many filing systems consist largely of folders standing laterally on shelves. The idea of hanging files has caught on only for drawer files. In Europe, however, lateral suspended files are very common; they offer the advantage of easier handling than the system of standing lateral filing used in the United States. Lateral suspended folders require a little more space due to their suspension device, and the file folders of lateral suspended filing systems are more expensive than shelf lateral filing, but the housing, that is, the cabinets and shelving units, are less expensive because no shelves or shelf dividers are required. Shelves are replaced by suspension rails. It is amazing that none of the manufacturers of color coded filing systems have introduced lateral suspended filing, as it facilitates straight alignment of color bars. This increases the value of color coding substantially.

Fasteners

Every records manager has to deal with the question of whether paper should be kept loose within the folder (the most common kind of record container) or secured by a fastener. The traditional rule of thumb was that once the folder held more than 20 pages of paper permanently, a fastener was installed in the folder to secure the paper and to keep the pages in chronological sequence. Today it is a question of internal organization. Legal documents, medical documents, and documents of similar importance are secured within the file folder even when there are only a few sheets of paper. In other applications it seems to be common to store in excess of an inch of paper in a file folder without securing the paper by a fastener. Typical examples are files of accounting applications, unfinished correspondence folders, and general "small business" folders.

A records manager has a choice of various styles for fasteners in the file folder. Many file clerks complain about the old metal fasteners, which cut fingers and paper and make it almost impossible to insert new pages into the middle of the stack of paper. Photocopying a page within a full file folder necessitates either losing the margin of the page or extracting the paper and then realigning and rethreading it. It is amazing that in our world of photo-copying no better fastening device has been offered.

The Acco clip, a metal fastener available in various lengths, is the most commonly used fastener throughout the United States. Metal clips are often used in connection with a metal compressor bar, which acts like a bridge between the two prongs. This is quite common in law firms. To avoid damage of folder covers, some manufacturers have fasteners that are heat-sealed into the file folder. Remclip from Remington Rand was the first fastener of this type; Permclip is another style. Heat sealing means that these fasteners cannot be attached to the file folder by the user, but only in file folder factories with the help of special heat-sealing machines. Alternatively, pressure-sensitive metal fasteners are available to be glued into the file folder. However, heat-sealed fasteners are more permanently attached to the file folder than are pressure-sensitive fasteners, which later may became unstuck if left on a windowsill or exposed to heat.

To overcome the disadvantages of sharp metal edges, plastic-coated fasteners are available. However, they are very expensive and therefore have been more successful in Europe than in the United States. European filing companies were also the first to produce and market plastic fasteners. Since the early 1960s, various European filing companies have offered more than five different types of plastic fasteners. Only one made it with reasonable success to the United States. The Ames Easiclip, a pressure-sensitive version of the German Schlauchheftung, was first introduced in the United States in 1977 by Ames Color File Corporation, a Boston-based firm, which marketed it initially only to the medical market.[3]

When Ames Color File Corporation was merged with Ames Safety Envelope Company, this fastener became available to the nonmedical record management field. Easiclip consists of a flexible plastic tube, an extension piece, and a bulky compressor bar. This arrangement gives the ring binder effect. Easiclip costs are often twice those of a conventional metal fastener, sometimes even more. Its second disadvantage is its compressor bar, which has a closing mechanism that is bulky and wastes space. This is probably Easiclip's biggest disadvantage when one considers the space shortage every records manager has to face. Finally, if only a page or a couple of pages are filed on top of the file, Easiclip slows the operation down. In order to add one piece of paper to the top of the stack, one has to unhook the tube, move the compressor bar to the end of the extension piece, and pull the extension piece off the tube. After the sheet has been inserted, one has to follow the same steps in reverse.

A second plastic fastener was introduced by the Eldon Company of California, a company well known in the field of plastic office products. Their fastener is called Elfast and works like a conventional metal fastener except that it is plastic and therefore protects paper and fingers. To install it into a folder or binder one has to punch holes into the outer cover and thread the fastener from the back through the cover. Elfast, introduced in 1979-80 to the market, is available through the stationery trade.

Another plastic fastener is Nuclip,[4] a pressure-sensitive plastic fastener that tries to match the advantages of Easiclip, namely, easy photocopying and the possibility of inserting or extracting into or from the middle without the cumbersome exercise of taking all the papers off the fastener, then realigning them and threading them again onto the fastener (see Plate 2.15). Nuclip is designed as a one-piece fastener that does not take up more space than a conventional metal fastener. The fastener offers the advantage of protecting the folder, its paper contents, and file clerks' hands because of its smooth all-plastic design. It also allows a folder to be used like a ring binder. One can photocopy a full page without losing the margin because the fastener creates an arch. Papers can be moved to the left. Its unique design allows the ends of the prongs to be bent, even into a T position, which acts as a stop. Papers moved to the left for the purpose of photo-copying, will not come loose because the prongs, with their ends bent into a T position, will stop papers from sliding off the fastener. After photo-

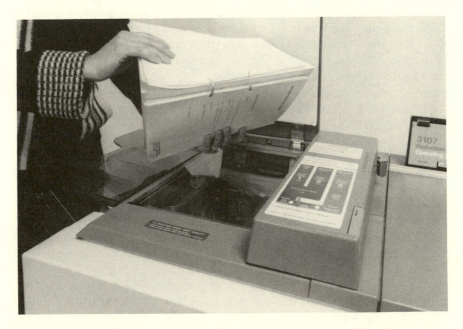

2.15   Plastic fastener allowing photocopying without losing margins or having to extract pages. Courtesy Nuclip Corp.

copying the ends of the fastener can be bent back into locking position (see Plates 2.16 and 2.17). This makes it possible to photocopy a full page without removing the page from the folder. To insert or extract from the middle of the stack one adds an additional Nuclip to the fastener by clipping the channeled prongs together. One prong is channeled and thus is designed to accept the second prong according to the zip-lock principle so common with plastic bags.

Once the pages are moved onto the added clip, one can select the point at which a page is to be extracted. Pulling the two clips apart creates an open-

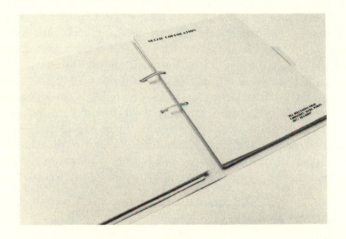

2.16   Nuclip fastener in closed and locked position. Courtesy Nuclip Corp.

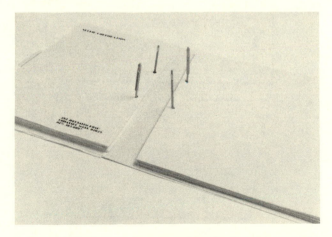

2.17   Nuclip fastener in open position for insertion or extraction of paper. Courtesy Nuclip Corp.

ing, which enables the file clerk to extract or insert documents into the file. The prongs will hold up to 50 pages securely in the file folder when bent down like metal prongs into an open position. This is a time-saving feature. For more than 50 pages one can close the fastener by snapping the two prongs together. This way, over an inch capacity can be held together. For security the two prongs can be interlocked, thereby making sure that the fasteners do not open accidentally.

Nuclip saves space in comparison with Easiclip, and its costs are only a little higher than those of the traditional metal fastener. It is pressure-sensitive so it can be installed by the end user. Its adhesive is tested to hold the full weight of a thick file folder. All plastic fasteners in the United States have 2.75-inch (7-centimeter) hole distance and often have only up to 1 inch or 1.5 inches capacity. Metal fasteners are available for more capacity. File companies have standard numbers for positions of fasteners. The trend seems toward an increased use of the fifth position (see Plate 2.18).

The next question in selecting a folder or binder is the material. Most folder companies offer a choice of materials—11-point, 13-point, and so on. The anticipated wear and retention period must be considered when selecting material. Stronger material is available for expansion files. Good results have been achieved by using Tyvec material to strengthen folders. Files made of plastic have not been successful in any major market (yet) although

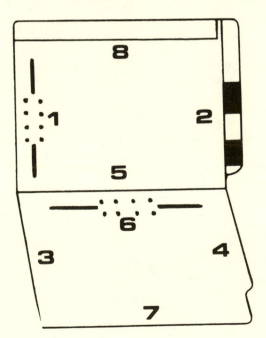

2.18   Standard fastener positions. Courtesy Colortrieve, Inc.

they are very durable. Plastic folders and binders slide off each other very easily so they cannot be stacked, and the fact that they break easily has been especially discouraging. I am sure that some of these problems can be eliminated as new materials become available.

The following questions should be considered in selecting document container design:

1. Are documents to be kept loose or secured within a file folder?

2. What kind of stock is required?

3. What kind of storage system is or will be used (shelf file, hanging file, or lateral file)?

4. What printing is required?

5. Which size suits the documents best?

6. Which indexing and at which side (top or side) is best?

Indexing at the top is, of course, very popular with drawer files. Indexing at the side, however, is becoming more prevalent, especially in most larger systems. The most efficient indexing for lateral filing is color coding.

Color Coding

Color coding eliminates misfiling and speeds up the search process. It was introduced in the late 1950s, when companies learned to print two or three color bars to a reinforced, outstanding edge of the folder or wallet. By printing large quantities and sorting them, a continuing numerical sequence was achieved. This meant also that folders could be supplied "preindexed" and the user did not have to go through the process of indexing numbers or colors on each individual file folder. The idea caught on, particularly with the spread of terminal digital filing systems. These divide a file in advance into 100 file stations and use terminal digits for indexing within each file station. In continuous filing systems, terminal digital filing means that a system can be balanced throughout the complete system (see Plate 2.19). With these 100 file stations it works out in many applications that approximately half a shelf is color-coded with the same two or three color bars. Misfiling would only be undetected if it happened within that half-shelf of folders with the same color coding.

Companies like TAB soon extended the system to more digits and were able to process interrupted systems. Acme Visible Records, Inc., and other companies developed the system of color coding for alphabetical indexing. At the beginning of the 1980s over 25 companies marketed color-coded filing systems in various styles. Their designs range from the traditional two- or three-color scheme to indexing with six or even eight color bands. A computer-generated color indexing system was developed by TAB and

Terminal digit is a method of filing numbers not issuing numbers. Numbers may be issued numerically or randomly but are filed in 100 terminal digit patterns. It's analogous to a new automobile's speedometer, which issues numbers sequentially; we'll just spread the wheels a bit.

A new car's speedometer looks like this ▶ ─────────────────

Let's now separate the wheels or digits into pairs and name them. The last two wheels at the right are the Terminal Digits.

The first mile driven (first patient) is 00-00-01 and is filed in the 01 terminal digit (TD) section of the file below.

The second mile (or patient) is 02 and is filed in the 02 section; etc. thru number 99, which goes in the 99 TD section. ─────────

The speedometer makes a trip around the file room every 100 patients. The 100th patient moves the last two wheels to 00 again while the third wheel changes from 0 to 1. This patient is filed in TD section 00, but we now divide into 100 sections 00-99 according to the middle digits. Patient 100 (00-01-00) has middle digits 01 and is filed to the extreme left therefore. The wheel continues until No. 1 99 and the speedometer has made another trip around the fileroom. The next patient number 200, (00-02-00) is filed in TD section 00 but to the right of patient 100 (00-01-00) according to middle digits. Ultimately patient 5000 (00-50-00) is filed in TD section 00 but in the center according to middle digits.

This process continues until your 10,000 file area is full. Then pick any TD section, eg. 99, and you find that the middle digit pairs progress from 00 to 99 within TD 99. Patient 9,999 (00-99-99) is filed in TD 99 section on the far right. The next patient 10,000 (01-00-00) is in TD section 00 but goes at the extreme left according to the middle digits. Now this middle section is sub divided into 100 sections 00-99 according to the tertiary digits of the patient number.

After passing 10,000 the tertiary digits are referred to (01-99-99) and similarly progress from 00 to 99 within their middle digit specific section.

When your file area is full, simply purge by oldest date of last activity. Make a complete trip around the file room and remove files to remote area (staying in TD order). Result: Space is utilized at near capacity on continuing basis with only **active** patients. A well purged and uncrowded file area is the most efficient and color coding enhances the entire operation in dramatically efficient ways.

TERMINAL DIGIT SECTIONS — 10,000 patients

2.19   Terminal digital description. Courtesy Colortrieve, Inc.

Datafile. Generally, the trend is away from printing. Records managers prefer individual labels that are attached automatically and often are coated with mylar, a transparent plastic cover that protects the colors, but the wide range of color coding systems and products may be confusing to many records managers.

The main criterion for selecting a number of color bars or labels is the volume of the file. Obviously, a system with 20,000 file folders should not have six color labels for identification. Such a system should have no more than three colors, bringing the average section with the same color coding to 20 file folders. Four colors would mean that on average there are only 2 folders with the same color coding. In practice, then, in many cases no folder or only one folder would have a specific color coding. When almost each folder is color-coded differently, the lack of consistency makes the system too confusing. Five or six color bands mean that there is *theoretically* less than one folder per color station, and color coding loses its usefulness. To work out how many color bars you require, keep in mind that each color represents one digit of your volume. Deduct the first two or three digits to arrive at the suggested number of color bands or color labels. Each digit stands for one color band. Here is an example: You want 50 folders per code out of a volume of 50,000. The 3 digits behind 50 mean that you require three color bands. Some of the major companies have developed their own color scheme and specific label/color band size in order to lock customers into repeat buying. But there are competitive companies for every color coding system on the market, and it is worthwhile for every records manager to shop around for the best price and service.

Computer-Readable Indexing

To prepare for the future, you should have some computer-readable indexing on the binder or folder cover. For the operation of a computer-controlled record control system it is helpful to print the file number or the index characters on the folder. The printed computer-readable index can then be scanned by a special device. Arthur Fitzgerald and Jack Goldman developed in the early 1970s the "guiding light system," a computer-controlled record control system using bar code technology and a light pen for scanning. This system was marketed by Ames Color File Corporation to medical institutions.

Ames's guiding light system was never that successful, and the company retreated in 1979 to marketing the light pen terminals only. Users had to design their own software and were given very little help with hardware outside of the pen terminals and related equipment. However, the company convinced many medical institutions to print bar codes on folders and X-ray jackets.

There is nothing wrong with planning ahead and putting a computer-readable index on the folder cover. Record trace systems are still not popular enough, but they will be a major tool for controlling hard copy with the help of a computer. It is the first step toward computerization of the file in many file rooms. By printing that index on the folder cover now, a records manager can be prepared for this future technology. However, one has to be careful when deciding which computer-readable code to print. First, if one decides on bar code technology, care must be taken in choosing a bar code language. There are a number of bar code languages available, and the key to selecting the right kind of language lies in knowing the computer equipment to be used for that operation.

For example, in an organization where the data processing manager was trained on IBM equipment and states openly that his "organization will always use IBM equipment," then the records manager should look into IBM bar code or OCR systems and specify the index to the file folder manufacturer. This may be an exaggeration, but communication with the management, data processing department, or whoever one considers informed on future directions of the data processing organization may provide clues as to which way to go.

In the past, bar codes were the most reliable method of automated data capture. A new technology, called optical character recognition (OCR), has not only caught up but is most promising for future applications. OCR codes are computer-readable letters and numbers that humans can read, too. See chapter 5 for more information on data capture. Most OCR scanners can read typefaces like prestige elite, courier 72, letter gothic, prestige pica, courier 12, pica 72, elite 72, advocate, delegate, and adjutant—basically any typeface produced on any typewriter (see Plate 2.20). By printing the document number in OCR, the problems of bar code language selection can be avoided. There is no question that OCR data capture will be the technology of the future. Actually, companies like Datafile Ltd. have already developed stand-alone record trace systems in OCR technology.

2.20   Record trace computer terminal with OCR scanner. Courtesy Datafile Ltd.

Guide to Increases in Filing Capacity Using
Alternate Storage Equipment in Place of
Four-Drawer Letter-Size Cabinets

Five-drawer cabinet	20%
Letter-sized lateral file, open shelving type	
5-tier	60%
6-tier	89%
7-tier	118%
8-tier	146%
Letter-sized lateral file, enclosed with doors, 6-tier	43%
Times-two cabinet	
5-tier, stand-alone	49%
5-tier, as add-on unit	71%
6-tier, stand-alone	75%
6-tier, as add-on unit	102%
7-tier, stand-alone	101%
7-tier, as add-on unit	133%
8-tier, stand-alone	128%
8-tier, as add-on unit	164%
Power files	
14 carriers	79%
16 carriers	102%
18 carriers	125%
Lateral mobile shelving, 2-tier	
6 shelves	158%
7 shelves	198%
8 shelves	238%
Lateral mobile shelving, 3-tier	
6 shelves	218%
7 shelves	268%
8 shelves	318%
Vertical mobile shelving, 6-foot sections, 4 sections per aisle	
6 shelves	202%
7 shelves	256%
8 shelves	305%
Vertical mobile shelving, 9-foot sections, 4 sections per aisle	
6 shelves	239%
7 shelves	294%
8 shelves	336%

NOTES

1. Robert P. Gilotte, "Circular Filing vs. Linear Filing," *ARMA Quarterly* 16, no. 3 (July 1982): 18-20.

2. It is true that certain objects like papers clips increase the bulk of documents somewhat. However, such increase depends on the number of clips, staples, or other devices. The author considers the average increase of such bulky items to be less than what Mr. Gilotte claims.

3. It was the author of this book who convinced the president of Ames Color File Corporation to introduce this fastener to the United States, subsequently acting as vice-president responsible for its development and adaptation to the U.S. market.

4. Developed and patented by the author, who is also president of Nuclip Corporation of Boston, Massachusetts.

3

COST MANAGEMENT

LABOR COSTS

At first glance it seems impossible to develop general guidelines of cost management that are applicable to all record systems. Every system seems to be different in layout, activity, volume, and space occupied. For further analysis we have to break down various cost components.

Labor costs, being a combination of clerical costs and supervision, is a major part in any record department's budget. Labor costs depend on the activity level, retrieval procedure, volume, and kinds of supplies and equipment used. Volume and activity level are given factors that cannot be changed, but the records manager has some influence over the retrieval procedure. Also supplies, such as file folders and document containers, are selected by the records manager, who should consider that different types of containers will influence the time spent filing and/or retrieving documents. Labor costs are in direct relationship to efficiency levels, for which supplies and equipment are major components. To analyze labor costs of document containers and equipment, we have to break the costs down into the following elements: (1) equipment accessing time; (2) document container accessing time; (3) document inserting time; (4) document restoring time; and (5) equipment restoring time.

For example, a document is to be filed into a drawer cabinet. Category 1 includes the time spent walking to the cabinet, finding the right cabinet, and opening the drawer. Category 2 is the time spent finding the required document container within the drawer; category 3 combines the time spent inserting the document into the wallet, if it is a hanging wallet-type file, and/or the time spent extracting the binder from the drawer and inserting the document into the fastener, if the paper is secured by a fastener.

Category 4 is the inserting of the binder back to the right place within the drawer, and category 5 is the closing of the drawer and walking back to the desk. Each category should be considered when buying equipment and supplies. Category 1 is related to how space efficient the selected equipment is. Obviously, equipment that makes better use of space also cuts walking distances and therefore labor costs. When designing a filing system, the records manager should consider distances from desks or requesting stations to the file housings (cabinets). Lateral shelving is time and labor saving for categories 1 and 2 but may take more time in category 3 than drawer filing systems. Of course, only the comparison of actual filing (adding documents to the file) and retrieval will yield true figures. It is easy to decide that documents are to be kept loose within a hanging pocket until the figures for searching during retrieval are added. The outcome may be that it is better and cheaper to keep documents secured with a fastener because then all documents will be in chronological order. To give a few examples of how long it takes to insert documents into a record, in one day (full shift), one can insert 700 documents into a loose file,[1] 500 documents into a file using a traditional metal fastener,[2] 250-350 documents into a file with Easiclip,[3] and 350-400 documents into a file with Nuclip.[4] Table 3.1 shows how activities break down by equipment categories.

Companies producing color-coded filing systems claim 25 percent savings in labor cost and an increase in productivity. Users of color coding have confirmed faster retrieval and less time-consuming misfiling. For instance, for insurance applications, Datafile claims a savings of 40 percent of space costs by converting from drawer cabinets to lateral files. An additional 25 percent of the clerical cost is saved, representing categories 1 and 2. They claim that this figure already includes the increase in labor in category 3

3.1 Filing Rates Using Various Equipment

Equipment	References per Hour	File Actions per Employee Day
Vertical files	25-35	280
Lateral files	39-40	320
Open shelf files	30-40	320
Vertical mobile shelving	25-35	280
Automated shelving with individual container section (Minitrieve)	50-60	480

Source: Supreme Equipment and Systems Corporation, "Office Productivity: The Strategies of Filing," Brooklyn, N.Y., 1980.

(pulling the record from the shelf and inserting the paper). This means that conversion to lateral shelving with the combination of color coding can save 18.4 percent of the total budget.[5]

However, when considering a conversion to lateral filing and color coding, the records manager should not forget to include the cost of capital spending. This is an area where filing companies leave questions unanswered, as is the cost of training and of indexing new files (see Plate 3.1). Information gets even less definite in the sphere of retrieval costs. costs. Without exact data on information flow, information retrieval type, frequency, and processing, it is difficult to compute retrieval costs with any precision.

STORAGE COSTS

The one area where we can develop general cost formulas applicable to any kind of equipment or installation is storage. Here we consider the cost of storing documents in document containers for a given retention period. Record storage costs depend on (1) equipment and supplies, (2) space occupied, and (3) cost of space (the kind of building, etc.). For comparison purposes it is useful to compute the cost per LFF per year, which can be done in three steps:

STEP 1: COST OF FILING EQUIPMENT + COST OF SUPPLIES = COST OF MATERIALS

To determine the cost of materials we must know the costs of equipment and supplies per linear filing foot (LFF). How can we get the cost of equipment per LFF? If new equipment is purchased, the quotation from a prospective vendor should state the cost in terms of LFFs. Sometimes it is stated as cost per LFI, which can be converted into cost per LFF by multiplying the data by 12. For instance, the purchase price of a four-drawer cabinet, which has a capacity of 100 LFIs, may be $100,* so the cost of equipment per LFI is 100:100, or $1. Multiplying that figure by 12, we arrive at $12 as the cost per LFF. To calculate the cost of existing equipment for which the purchase price is unknown, take 30-40 percent of the cost of a new system as basis for this computation.

Once you have the cost of your housing per LFF, you will want to establish the cost of supplies per LFF. First, find out how many folders/binders/containers there are in your system per LFF. The best way to get this data is to count the number of folders, binders, or pockets you have in one drawer or on one shelf. Select a drawer or shelf with typical folder/binder/container thickness and average loading conditions. Then divide the number of containers by the number of LFIs and multiply the result by 12

*This figure is not meant as a guideline for drawer cabinet costs.

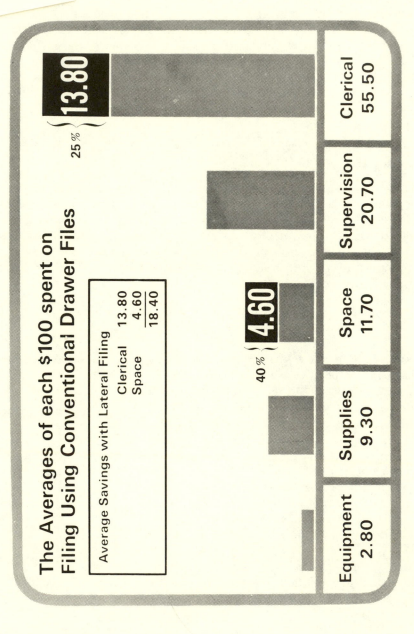

The Averages of each $100 spent on Filing Using Conventional Drawer Files

25% } **13.80**

Average Savings with Lateral Filing

Clerical	13.80
Space	4.60
	18.40

40% } **4.60**

Equipment	Supplies	Space	Supervision	Clerical
2.80	9.30	11.70	20.70	55.50

3.1   Comparison of filing costs. Courtesy Datafile Ltd.

for the number of records per LFF. If, for example, there are 50 records in a 25-inch drawer, then there are 24 records per LFF (50:25 = 2, 2 × 12 = 24). Or if you have 90 records on a 3-foot-wide shelf, then there are 30 records per LFF (90/3 = 30).

Next we have to establish the cost of filing supplies per LFF, that is, the cost of folders, binders, pockets, and any other kind of document containers, including divider sheets, labels, fasteners, inner pockets, and special attachments. To do this, determine the cost of supplies per 1,000 records and then multiply that number by the number of records per LFF, as established above:

$$\frac{\text{Cost of unit}[6]}{\text{unit}} \times \text{number of records} = \text{cost of materials}$$

If we assume that the cost of supplies is $400 per $1,000 records and that there are 50 records per LFF, then the cost of supplies per LFF is $20 ($400 ÷ 1,000 × 50).

By adding the cost of equipment per LFF to the cost of supplies per LFF we can compute the cost of materials per LFF. Thus, if the cost of equipment is $12 per LFF and the cost of supplies is $20 per LFF, then the cost of materials is $32 per LFF.

STEP 2: (SPACE-EFFICIENCY FACTOR × COST OF
ESTATE) + COST OF REAL ESTATE
SERVICE = SPACE COST PER LFF
PER YEAR

It costs money to occupy space, and real estate costs are increasing every year. Even if your organization owns its building you should be aware of the accounting costs for the space occupied by the record system. After all, if that space were not used for records, it could be used for another purpose or leased.

As stated earlier, the amount of space occupied depends on its layout, the volume, and the equipment. The records manager usually cannot do much about the volume, as this is created by the organization. The only way to influence the volume is by changing the retention schedule which may be difficult, if not impossible. The area where the records manager can monitor the space occupied by the record system is equipment selection.

Various equipments have different space efficiencies. This means that when storing a given capacity one type of filing equipment uses more space than another. Low equipment, like drawer cabinets and counter-high cabinets and shelves, has a low space efficiency. Three categories of space efficiency can be identified: low, intermediate, and high.

Low space efficiency covers equipment with factors over 1.0. The range of equipment in this category is from the two-drawer cabinet (2.93, if placed singularly), to the letter-size three-tier lateral file which is counter high and has a space efficiency factor of 1.17 (placed singularly). Intermediate space efficiency is attributed to the five-drawer letter-size cabinet with a factor of .98 (singularly) to the seven-tier letter-size lateral file with a factor of .50 (singularly). High efficiency of space starts under .50 and peaks around and under .20, with the lowest figure (see the list below) for vertical mobile shelving, eight tiers high, with 12-feet-deep sections and four sections per aisle. This factor could be decreased by adding more sections to the system per aisle and extending the length of the sections.[7] As you can see, the lower the space-efficiency factor the better the space efficiency.

Space Efficiency Factors

	File Placed Singularly			File Sharing an Aisle		
	Sq. Ft.	LFFs	Space Efficiency Factor	Sq. Ft.	LFFs	Space Efficiency Factor
Low efficiency						
2-drawer, legal-size cabinet	11.75	4	2.93	9.37	4	2.34
2-drawer, letter-size cabinet	9.75	4	2.43	7.87	4	1.96
3-drawer, legal-size cabinet	11.75	6	1.95	9.37	6	1.56
3-drawer, letter-size cabinet	9.75	6	1.62	7.87	6	1.31
4-drawer insulated security cabinet	12.75	8	1.62	10.37	8	1.29
4-drawer, legal-size cabinet	11.75	8	1.46	9.37	8	1.17
4-drawer, letter-size cabinet	9.75	8	1.21	7.87	8	.98
5-drawer, legal-size cabinet	11.75	10	1.18	9.37	10	.94
3-tier, counter-high, lateral file	10.50	9	1.17	6.75	9	.75
Intermediate efficiency						
5-drawer, letter-size cabinet	9.75	10	.98	7.87	10	.79
5-tier, X-ray open shelf or legal file with doors	12.00	15	.80	8.25	15	.55
Minitrieve (Supreme), letter-size, with work station M/T 0903	143.00	202	.71			
5-tier, circular rotary file Giro-oblique	14.00	20	.70			
(If inner space is taken into account [50%])	14.00	30	.46			
6-tier, legal-size lateral file	12.00	18	.66	8.25	18	.45
6-tier, letter-size file	10.50	18	.58	6.75	18	.37
7-tier, lateral file with Databoxes	10.50	19	.55	6.75	19	.35
7-tier, letter-size file	10.50	21	.50	6.75	21	.32
8-tier, open-shelf, letter-size, lateral file	10.50	24	.43	6.75	24	.28

	File Placed Singularly			File Sharing an Aisle		
	Sq. Ft.	LFFs	Space Efficiency Factor	Sq. Ft.	LFFs	Space Efficiency Factor
High-density storage-high space efficiency						
Times Two or Rotomatic, letter-size						
5-shelf high, stand-alone	15.90	20.8	.76	11.96	20.8	.57
5-shelf, as add-on unit	13.56	20.8	.65	10.18	20.8	.49
6-shelf, stand-alone	15.90	25	.64	10.18	25	.48
6-shelf, as add-on unit	13.56	25	.54	10.18	25	.41
7-shelf, stand-alone	15.90	29.2	.55	11.96	29.2	.41
7-shelf, as add-on unit	13.56	29.2	.46	10.18	29.2	.35
8-shelf, stand-alone	15.9	33.3	.48	11.96	33.3	.36
8-shelf, as add-on unit	13.56	33.3	.41	10.18	33.3	.31
Power files						
14 carriers	63.75	102.83	.62	53.2	102.8	.52
16 carriers	63.75	117.5	.54	53.2	117.5	.45
18 carriers	63.75	132.2	.48	53.2	132.2	.40
Minitrieve, letter-size, including work station						
M/T 0909	284.00	607	.47			
M/T 0915	363.00	1015	.36			
M/T 0920	451.00	1350	.33			
M/T 0925	439.00	1687	.26			
Lateral letter-size, mobile shelving, Bifile or similar						
6-shelf, 2 tiers	15.00	36	.41	11.25	36	31
7-shelf, 2-tiers	15.00	42	.35	11.25	42	.26
8-shelf, 2-tiers	15.00	48	.31	11.25	48	.23
Trifile or similar						
6-shelf, 3-tiers	18.00	54	.33	15.75	54	.29
7-shelf, 3-tiers	18.00	63	.28	15.75	63	.25
8-shelf, 3-tiers	18.00	72	.25	15.75	72	.21
Vertical mobile shelving, X-ray-size or oversized, 18 inches deep, 5 shelves high, 3 double sections per aisle						
3 feet deep	64.63	90	.72	49.94	90	.55
6 feet deep	97.75	180	.54	83.37	180	.46
9 feet deep	132.25	270	.48	117.87	270	.43
12 feet deep	166.75	360	.46	152.37	360	.42
Vertical mobile shelving, letter-size, 6 shelves						
3 feet deep	48.12	108	.44	37.18	108	.34
6 feet deep	74.37	216	.34	63.45	216	.29

	File Placed Singularly			File Sharing an Aisle		
	Sq. Ft.	*LFFs*	*Space Efficiency Factor*	*Sq. Ft.*	*LFFs*	*Space Efficiency Factor*
9 feet deep	100.62	324	.31	89.68	324	.27
12 feet deep	126.87	432	.29	115.93	432	.26
Vertical mobile shelving, letter-size, 7 shelves						
3 feet deep	48.12	126	.38	37.18	126	.29
6 feet deep	74.37	252	.29	63.45	252	.25
9 feet deep	100.62	378	.26	89.68	378	.24
12 feet deep	126.87	504	.25	115.93	504	.23
Vertical mobile shelving, letter-size, 8 shelves						
3 feet deep	48.12	144	.33	37.18	144	.26
6 feet deep	74.37	288	.26	63.45	288	.22
9 feet deep	100.62	432	.23	89.68	432	.21
12 feet deep	126.87	576	.22	115.9	576	.20

Aisle space is a major component of space costs, so it makes a difference whether cabinets or files share a common aisle. Therefore, the space-efficiency factor is always higher for files placed singularly. Files placed opposite each other, sharing a common aisle between them, have a lower space-efficiency factor, as shown above in the right column. For comparison purposes it is usually all right to use the factor for singularly placed files. When the layout of prospective equipment is known, it is advisable to use the appropriate space-efficiency factor. For some types of equipment this may even be a combination of singularly placed and sharing equipment, of stand-alone and add-on equipment.

To establish the cost of space occupied by the record system, you have to establish the value of the space occupied, that is, the yearly cost of occupying space by the square foot. Of course, these data vary greatly according to the condition and value of the building and also the location. Differences in annual space costs per square foot between urban and rural areas are also substantial.

However, you should get the cost of space for your area or, even better, for your building from the house management, accounting, budgeting, or real estate department. This figure, given in dollars per square foot, should be adjusted every year to account for inflation and fluctuating real estate prices. Taking the annual real estate cost per square foot and multiplying it by the space-efficiency factor yields the base cost of space per LFF. For instance, if the annual real estate costs are $10 per square foot and you are using seven-tier open shelving, the space costs per LFF is $5 ($10 × .50, the appropriate space-efficiency factor). But to capture the space costs, we have to include the cost of services in addition to the real estate costs. Cost of services is the ongoing costs for lighting, cleaning, air conditioning, heating, painting, and repairs to that space.

Unfortunately, there are no detailed guidelines for establishing the cost of services, and each record room has different requirements in regard to these services, so the cost factor will be different. Experience has shown that these costs of services range from 10 percent to 50 percent of annual real estate costs. The cost range of 30-50 percent of real estate costs applies only to records kept in "office condition," that is, when carpeting, air conditioning, and other "luxury office conditions" are used in the area where records are kept. Most record rooms are in the bracket of 10-30 percent for service costs. A record room in the basement, serviced just by lighting and cleaning, is usually in the 5-20 percent range. Air conditioning adds another 10-30 percent. The records manager has to have an educated guess of service costs for the area occupied by record storage equipment.

To compute the cost of space, take this percentage of the annual real estate costs per square foot, which represents the cost of services, and add it to the annual real estate costs. For instance, if the real estate costs are $10 per year per square foot and the cost of services is estimated at 25 percent, then the space costs are $12.50 ($10 + [25% × 10] = $12.50).

Now we can proceed to the computation of annual storage costs per LFF.

STEP 3: COST OF MATERIALS/YEARS OF STORAGE + SPACE COSTS = STORAGE COSTS

The cost of record storage per year per LFF is determined by dividing the cost of materials by the number of years of storage and adding to that the space costs. By multiplying the cost of storage by the total number of LFFs in a filing system, you can compute the total cost of storage.

This figure does not include any retrieval cost (searching and pulling a record). However, it is very helpful to compare different types of equipment and various storage options with respect to their costs. Every records manager should know the cost of storage for her or his filing system. The figure should be updated annually to reflect changes in the costs of real estate and other factors.

The next question is how long records are going to be kept in this area. This is not to be mistaken for the retention period. Rather, we may want to compute the cost of an active file area. Then only the period of storage in this particular file is to be considered for the computation. When records are kept for less than seven years, the equipment outlasts the records.

To derive the annual cost of short- and medium-term storage (all in terms of LFFs), assuming that equipment lasts ten years and the time in storage is less than seven years (a generally accepted assumption for accounting and depreciation purposes), we have the following formula:

$$\text{cost of equipment}/10 + \text{cost of supplies}/\text{years of storage}$$
$$= \text{storage costs}$$

Remember that the cost of storage provides cost figures on equipment, supplies, and space but does not give clerical, supervision, or retrieval costs. It is simply the cost of storing records in certain equipment over a certain time. Also, filing costs are not included in the cost of storage.

Let us look at two examples of computing the cost of storage:

Exercise 1:

The record department has open lateral shelving with 7 tiers. The shelving has a 50 percent purchase value. New shelving of the same kind would cost $1 per LFI. There are 30 records on one shelf, and each shelf is 3 feet long, so there are 10 records per foot. File folders cost $380 per thousand. The cost of space is $6 per square foot per year. Services are estimated at 15 percent of the cost of space. Records are to be kept in this room for 20 years.

First, to convert the cost of shelving from cost per LFI to cost per LFF, multiply 0.40 by 12, which is 4.80. Next, compute the cost of materials per LFF, by adding the costs of shelving and supplies:

$$4.80 + 3.80 = 8.60$$

Now, to compute the yearly space charges, multiply the annual real estate cost per square foot by the space-efficiency factor, which for this type of equipment is .50, and to it add 15 percent of that figure:

$$(.50 \times 6) + .15 \text{ x } (.50 \times 6) = 3.45$$

Thus, the total yearly space cost per LFF is $3.45.

Finally, to compute the yearly storage costs:

$$\frac{8.60}{20} + 3.45 = 3.88$$

The total storage cost per LFF per year in this case, then, is $3.88.

Exercise 2:

The department has the same data as in Exercise 1. It is running out of space but is legally obliged to keep records for three more years. It wants to establish the cost of keeping records on the existing shelving for three more years. Also, it has been established that if records were not kept in this room the existing shelving could not be used somewhere else.

What is the cost of storage per LFF per year?

For this case no new shelving is to be bought, nor can the old shelving be used somewhere else. File folders have been in use and could not be used for another application. There are practically no costs of materials. The cost of storage is limited to the cost of space, which is $3.45.

Selecting Filing Equipment

Although cost should not be the only factor considered when selecting filing equipment, in reality it is most often the main factor. Any vendor's estimate or quotation should state the cost of the equipment per LFI or per LFF. However, this is not the whole picture. We should always add the cost of space to the cost of equipment. It would be wonderful for prospective buyers if vendors stated the space-efficiency factor on each piece of literature. This would eliminate a lot of confusion. Users could compare equipment by its space efficiency. Also, records managers could compute in advance the storage cost of records for each optional equipment, as discussed above, by establishing the annual cost of real estate per square foot for the filing area and multiplying this figure by the space-efficiency factor for the given type of filing equipment. The true cost of filing equipment is the sum of the cost of equipment per LFF and the cost of space per LFF.

Let us look at an example.

The records manager is considering four-drawer cabinets versus lateral filing cabinets with six lockable tiers (no pullouts, doors retractable). An average price for the drawer cabinet is $175; for the lateral filing cabinet it is $380. The annual real estate costs for the office are in this case $16 per square foot. Services are estimated at an additional 25 percent, or $4 per square foot. Total costs of space, then, are $20 per square foot. What does the price comparison look like? The space-efficiency factor for the drawer cabinet is 1.62; for the lateral cabinet, .66.

There are 8.33 LFF in the four-drawer cabinet. The cost of equipment is $21 per LFF (175:8.33). The cost of space is $20 × 1.62 = $32.40. The total cost of these cabinets is $21 + $32.40 = $53.40 per LFF.

Now, let's take the lateral cabinet. It has six tiers and is three feet wide and so has a capacity of 18 LFF. The purchase price of $380 divided by 18 equals $21.11, the cost per LFF for material. Obviously, there is not much difference in the price of equipment between the drawer cabinet and the lateral filing cabinet. Yet when we look at space costs and include those in our costing, the picture changes. Multiplying the real estate costs of $20 times the space-efficiency factor, we get the space cost of $13.20 per LFF (20 × .66). The lateral cabinet costs only $34.31 per LFF, compared to the drawer cabinet, which costs $53.40 per LFF. The four-drawer cabinet actually costs 55 percent more when you include the space costs, although the purchase price seems to indicate that both types of filing equipment are almost equal in cost! Now you can multiply the difference times the number of LFF your new equipment is going to house and establish the savings or additional costs for each type of equipment.

Existing Versus Automated Equipment

To establish the cost of storage of existing shelving and compare it to proposed equipment, we proceed as follows. First, we establish the annual real estate costs for this particular filing area. After we obtain the annual cost per square foot for the location and type of building in which the filing system is to be housed, we multiply the number of square feet times the cost of space per square foot. The result is to be multiplied by the increase in capacity and provides an approximate gain from higher space efficiency which can be offset against capital outlay for new equipment.

Here is an example: The department is running out of space. The question is how to justify the purchase of new equipment. The records manager is looking into vertical mobile shelving, nine feet deep, seven shelves high, which could give an increase in capacity of 294 percent over the existing system (see page 48: listing of increase in capacity over four-drawer cabinets). The present system is housed in four-drawer cabinets with center aisles. The volume of the equipment with drawer cabinets is known to be 833 LFFs. At a 294 percent increase, the capacity of the proposed system is 3,283 LFFs. Of course, this increase is depending on the room layout and number of aisles. Therefore it is recommended to expect a 10 to 15 percent variation. The annual real estate costs are given in $10 per square foot.

What amount of capital can we spend to justify buying this kind of equipment? We can measure the floor area occupied and establish the number of square feet of the present filing system. Or, if we cannot do that (because a new building is involved, or files are merged), then we multiply the number of LFFs by the space-efficiency factor. For four-drawer cabinets, letter-sized, arranged on both sides of access aisles, the space-efficiency factor is .98. An area of approximately 800 square feet would be occupied by four-drawer files, holding 833 LFFs (833 $\times$ .98 = 816 square feet). Multiplying the 800 square feet by the $10 cost per square foot, we compute the annual space cost of the present system ($8,000). As the new proposed system has roughly three times the capacity of the old system, space costs for an expanded conventional system would be $24,000 per year. The decision of how many years should be taken to depreciate the equipment is up to management's discretion. However, it is generally accepted that mobile shelving lasts ten years. Also, the cost of money, usually averaged at 10 percent per year should be included in the financial comparison of capital outlay.

Off-site Storage

It is usually space shortage that forces an organization to rethink its plans for a record storage system. There are a number of ways to increase storage capacity using different equipment. In addition, the records manager has the choice of two outside possibilities. Off-site storage is one of these alternatives. It means taking advantage of low-cost space off site and then using the most cost-efficient equipment and supplies, particularly since the retrieval rate should be very low. The average figure for cost of off-site storage should be around $2 per year per LFF, however, in some cases these costs may go up to $4 per year per LFF. Again, this does not include retrieval costs. Commercial off-site storage companies charge between $1 and $10 per retrieval, depending on distance involved, retrieval schedule, and urgency. A recent survey stated the cost of an inactive storage facility as $0.02 to $1.00 per cubic foot per year.[8] Only one respondent reported significantly higher costs. Unfortunately, there was no distinction made in the survey between off-site storage and on-site storage. The survey included over 55 percent of inactive facilities storing records on site.

Microfilm

The second outside alternative is reducing records to microfilm. When we look at the possibility of microfilm, we should not just look at the storage value. The micrographics field offers a totally different information management tool. Its advantages are in the area of information handling and distribution, as well as in the area of storage. It is worthwhile to differentiate four different microfilm approaches.

In the first approach, information is generated on paper and is initially stored as hard copy. A retention period for hard copy is established, depending on availability of space. At the end of this retention period the information is microfilmed and stored on microfilm, mainly because there is not enough space to store all the hard copy records. When information is required, a hard copy print is made of the microfilm image for use by the information user.

Here we want to compare the cost of storage and examine microfilm in this aspect. Unfortunately, many executives resent dealing directly with microfilm in its original form and prefer hard copy records. This means that original paper records are created, sometimes also for legal or operational reasons. The paper documents are then stored until the organization starts running out of space. Then, for space reasons only, many organizations convert to microfilm.

In the second, information is generated on paper and is initially stored as hard copy. Lack of space forces the conversion to microfilm at the end of the hard copy period. However, from then on microfilm is usually not reconverted to hard copy. Microfilm readers are positioned throughout the organization. The original microfilm is kept in safe storage and copies are sent for reference or requests.

In the third, information is microfilmed at the beginning of the storage. No file folders or other document containers are used for this operation. Information is retrieved with microfilm readers.

In the last approach, information is generated on computers and recorded by computer output microfilm (COM) directly to microfilm and information is referenced by readers.

Let's look at the cost of each of these four applications.

Microfilm costs must be divided into conversion costs and storage costs. Conversion costs for in-house microfilming contain the costs of equipment, material, and labor. In the case of using an outside service bureau for the conversion to microfilm, there is usually a total charge for the whole job, except when in-house preparation—i.e., sorting, packing, preparing—has to be done by the records department.

Storage costs contain the equipment, the space, and possible preservation costs. The latter are often overlooked as a major part of microfilming. Unfortunately, the appropriate storage of microfilm under controlled conditions is not customary with many microfilm users. A proper preservation policy should be established by every records manager for the storage of microfilm.

In 1979, the Institute for Medical Record Economics surveyed microfilm users on the in-house cost of microfilming. The survey yielded the following costs for task man-hours per 100-foot film:

Make ready (all preparatory work)	3.5
Rotary filming	3.0
Processing	0.5
Inspection	0.7
Titles	1.8
Cut and insert in jackets	2.0
Sorting	0.5
Total man-hours	12.0

With variations of only 15 percent, most users agreed that they spent 12 man-hours on every film of 2,500 images. This means that the labor content of 12 hours at a rate of $6 per hour, including fringe benefits and supervisory costs, is $72.

For direct materials—film, chemicals, jackets, and so forth—users spent on the average another $18.75. For equipment use they stated only $13.13

per film, including maintenance. Thus in 1979 it did cost this user group on the average $43.75 to prepare one roll of film with 2,500 images, including labor and materials, and $86.25 to prepare 2,500 images, or one roll of film, and mount the film into jackets.

Another study compared in-house filming to contractors' costs.[9] In many cases microfilm service bureaus are specialized for processing large volume and can be more economical than any in-house operation. This study suggested only very basic equipment for in-house filming, namely, one rotary camera, one reader printer, and one reader. The cost figures were based on the following data: 80,000 film images filmed per year; sequencing rate at 1,000 images/pages per hour; removal/correction of impediments at 800 images per hour; placement of I.D. targets at 1,000 images/pages per hour; filming at 800 images/pages per hour; and inspection of images for quality control purposes at 1,000 per hour.

For the 80,000 images the following labor costs were assumed:

Preparation sequence	80 man-hours
Impediments	100 man-hours
I.D. targets	80 man-hours
Filming	100 man-hours
Inspection of film, quality control	80 man-hours
Total	440 man-hours

The average cost per man-hour is here assumed as $8. This figure includes fringe benefits, general and supervisory costs, and overhead costs. Thus the total labor cost is $3,520 (440 × $8). Of course, these data vary by location because pay scale, local circumstances, and the level of fringe benefits may vary. The records manager should feel free to insert the number that applies to her or his operation.

The second cost component is the cost of supplies and processing. This comprises the cost of materials including film and processing chemicals, and also depreciation of microfilming equipment.

Supplies and Processing

32 rolls of film @ $8.00	$256
Processing of 32 rolls @ $3.00	$96
Total	$352

The following equipment, used for in-house filming, has a straight five-year depreciation:

Camera @ $5,000	$1,000 per year
Reader/printer @ $3,200	$640 per year

Reader @ $1,400	$280 per year
Total	$1,920 per year

Therefore the total cost for equipment and supplies is $2,272 ($352 + $1,920).* By adding this figure to the total labor costs we get a total cost for filming 80,000 images of $5,792, or $72.40 per 1,000 images. These costs are for straight roll film. For jackets we have to add $20-40 per 1,000.

These individual studies show that, depending on application, equipment used, and microforms used, the conversion costs vary between $50 and $112 per 1,000 images. With different formats and equipment, a high figure of $200 can be reached.

How does microfilming fare in comparison with hard copy? As mentioned earlier, it is very difficult to establish figures combining retrieval and storage costs. Let us look first at the comparison of storage costs of originals (hard copy, X-ray films, etc.) and conversion costs of microfilm. We have seen that the storage of hard copy depends on material (equipment and supplies), cost of space, and length of storage. Most hard copy storage can be described as costing between $2 and $15 per LFF per year. Microfilm equipment storage costs consist of equipment space including environmental costs, labor costs for inspection, and other preservation costs (cleaning, etc.). Equipment costs are minimal, as we have some 20,000 (98 per fiche) images per inch. Even at a cost of $3 per LFI, the cost is under $0.20 per 1,000. Space costs are generally given at 2 percent of hard copy. However, for in-house applications we have to add the space for the microfilming equipment to the storage space. The storage space has to be controlled environmentally, which is quite costly.[10] Depending on the area involved and the condition of the building, the maintenance of that space may cost five to ten times more than regular space. Therefore, space costs for microfilm are about 20 percent of space costs for hard copy. Labor costs for preservation can be assumed at approximately $4 per 1,000. Adding all this up, we arrive at a storage figure of 12-20 percent of the storage costs of hard copy. The cost of reproducing microfilm into hard copy is usually given at $600 per thousand, including materials, labor, and overheads.

To compute a comparison for the first application, hard copy–microfilm–hard copy, we have to add the cost of conversion to microfilm ($50-112) to the cost of storage ($0.05-1.00). The conversion and storage cost excluding retrieval will be the cost of conversion divided by the number of years kept plus the cost of storage.

To compare microfilm to hard copy we have to break it down into comparable units, namely, linear filing feet. Approximately 2,500 sheets of paper, including in most cases even the folder covers, represent one LFF, which is comparable to 2,500 images of microfilm.

---

*The average department will require more than one reader.

The following comparison shows the annual cost of storage for hard copy, roll film, and microfilm jackets. The cost of hard copy varies between $.50 and $15 per LFF per year depending on the cost of space, equipment, and supplies, as well as storage period. The cost of roll film storage contains the cost of conversion to microfilm and preservation costs. For microfilm jackets the additional costs for rearranging images and feeding them into jackets has been added.

Comparison
Cost per Linear Filing Foot, Conversion Only
Storage Costs per LFF for 10 Years Storage

Per Year

Hard Copy	Roll Film	Jackets
$.50-15	$7-78	$16-124

In the first application the obvious differences between hard copy and microfilm will be magnified by even higher retrieval costs for microfilm (reproduction of hard copy). In the second application the savings in retrieval costs offset some of the high conversion costs, and the third application does better than break even, which means actual savings for the microfilm system. In the fourth application the picture is almost reversed: there are tremendous cost savings for microfilm.

Retrieval of hard copy is usually more expensive than retrieval of microfilm when executives are willing to use original microfilm. In the latter situation there are microfilm readers distributed throughout the organization, and microfilm information is generally not converted back to hard copy. As this shows, the key to the economical use of microfilm is the records manager's ability to convince management to use microfilm readers as retrieval tools.

However, in many applications of record storage, microfilm is used as a storage medium only. When someone wants information of that record, a print is made as a "working paper." In this case, microfilm is more expensive than hard copy. The federal government states that it can *store and reference* records for up to 70 years before it exceeds the cost of microfilming.[11] In federal storage centers records are kept at low space and storage costs. This is like off-site storage. Of course, each records manager has a different cost picture, since real estate costs, application requirements, and retrieval requirements vary from location to location.

In a study Gerald F. Brown shows the difference in costs of various microforms.[12] Although inflation has invalidated the final result for today's costing, it is interesting to compare the individual costs. The study seems

not to include cost of equipment or other related costs, but uses the cost of
the film (carrier) and labor (filming, not any of the other activities), taking
$5 as the labor cost unit. It gives the following costs per 1,000 images:

Roll film, 24X,[13] 100 feet, 16 mm

Rotary, handfed	$5.50
Autofed	$3.90
Planetary	$8.40
Jacket, 16 mm, 5 channel, 60 frames, rotary, handfed	$8.30
COM microfiche, 207 frames	$1.00

As the microfilm industry develops new, better, faster, and more reliable
equipment, microfilm becomes a more viable proposition. But the real
breakthrough can be expected with computer output microfilm (COM).

Computerized Storage of Information

At the time of the writing of this book hard copy storage is in many cases
still the most economical way of keeping information. In the 1960s the
slogan of the paperless office was born. Many office experts predicted that
paperless office technology would rule information storage in the 1980s, but
it did not come about as quickly as many people expected. The paperless
office slogan became linked to a call for less rather than more paper. The
paper-producing industry says that there was never as great a demand for
paper as during the early 1980s.

Computer costs have been reduced consistently. The prospect of bubble
memory seemed to be the breakthrough for economical magnetic information storage. It didn't happen. The data processing department stayed
faithful to its name: data processing is the computer's business, not data
storage. However, parts of the computer industry and affiliated industries
are working hard on a change. In 1977 it was assumed that computerized
storage of information was 200 times more expensive than microfilm. This
has changed drastically and continues to change. In 1982 and 1983 the first
signs of a new technology could be seen on the record storage horizon:
computer optical storage disks. Optical disk systems are still as expensive as
new. A large, high-performance drive for optical disks costs in 1982-83
$60-80,000, a disk in DRAW (Direct Read After Write) mode starts at
$1,000 or more. However, experts forecast a sales price of $200 for optical
disks storing 50,000 documents, or four-tenths of a penny per document.[14]
Others forecast optical disks at a price of $10 each, having a capacity of
6-10,000 images.

Presently, we can estimate the average storage cost for storage on magnetic
disk as $0.18 per page, microfilm (converted through COM) at $0.001-0.005
per page and optical storage (Raster Scan, five to one compaction) at

$0.002-0.006 per page. A retrieval device for microfilm costs between $200 and $10,000 + ; for magnetic disks, between $9,000 and $18,000.[15]

In all cases of computing the cost of storage we have to separate storage costs and conversion costs. Conversion costs are expenses incurred with the transition of information from one medium to another. When storage costs with a new medium are lower, we have to compare the savings in storage costs plus the one-time expenses of conversion to create the real cost picture.

All signs seem to indicate that optical disks will play a major part in information storage as they become economical and provide real competition for conventional storage.

NOTES

1. According to Louis Leitz Company, Stuttgart, Federal Republic of Germany.
2. Ibid.
3. According to the Institute for Medical Record Economics, Boston.
4. Ibid.
5. See brochure published by Datafile, Willowdale, Ontario, Canada: "The filing survey can pay off . . . handsomely," 1978.
6. A unit consists usually of 50, 100, or 1,000 pieces.
7. The most sections I have seen are fifteen per aisle in a very inactive and inaccessible vertical mobile filing system. The longest sections I have seen were over twenty-one meters (seventy feet) long.
8. Barbara A. Christensen, "An Analysis of Inactive Storage Facilities, Equipment, and Supplies," *ARMA Quarterly* (July 1982): 36-42.
9. "Understanding Microfilm: A Management Guide to Hospital Micrographics," Massachusetts Hospital Joint Ventures, Inc., 5 New England Executive Park, Burlington, MA 01803, 1977.
10. See the discussion of preservation policy in Chapter 4.
11. General Services Administration, National Archives and Records Services, Office of Records Management, *Records Management Handbook: Microfilming Records. Managing Information Retrieval*, U.S. Government Printing Office Nat. Stock no. 7610-00-387-9972 (Washington, D.C.: 1972).
12. Gerald F. Brown, *Microforms*, Readings on Records Management, Association of Records Managers and Administrators, no. 1514 (Prairie Village, Kans.: 1978).
13. X is the symbol for the reduction ratio in microfilming. 24X is a 24 times reduction ratio. (Original document is 1X, half that size would be 2X and so on.)
14. According to Mr. Edward J. Westlund, speaker for 3M Company at a debate at the International Micrographics Conference on September 13, 1982, in Copenhagen, Denmark.
15. See "The Mathematics of Filing: Cabinets vs. Electronics," *Administrative Management* (January 1982): 38-42.

4

MICROFILM

SYSTEMS OVERVIEW

It has been fascinating over the last three decades to watch the idea of microfilming grow into the technology of micrographics and into a philosophy for many micrographics fans. Developed during the mid-twentieth century, the micrographics industry has burgeoned into a successful, powerful, and attractive field. The idea of reducing the format of information carriers brought with it advantages in information handling, storing, and distributing. However, the key to the future success of micrographics is its ability to capture information produced by computers. This technology, computer output microfilm (COM), is more economical for information storage than computer output on hard copy (computer printouts) and, of course, much more economical than storage on magnetic media, at least at the time of writing this book. The challenge microfilm faced in the past remains: to convince executives in all kinds of organizations that they should use microfilm readers to retrieve and use information stored on microfilm.

Part of this battle is the quality of film produced on microfilm readers. Users are judging the quality of microfilm produced, the quality of the image on the reader display, and the convenience a reader offers. At present it looks as though the storage method of the future will be optical records, cut by laser in high density into disks. If this method proves to be as economical and safe as current predictions describe it, the microfilm industry will experience a major setback. But these predictions are not expected to become reality for many high-volume record storage applications before 1990 or even 1995.

What are the advantages of micrographics? There is no question that it can increase the operating efficiency in an office as it may overcome the growing resource requirements of systems that record and communicate information, and it may also improve the poor responsiveness of conventional systems. This means that it can make an information base more easily available and more usable.

On the negative side, you cannot just pick the microform up and read it. You need special equipment to read it and special equipment to produce it. You cannot update it easily, so you cannot write on it, and you have to provide special storage conditions for preservation.

An additional question may arise about the basic legality of microfilm for the planned application of transferring records or information to microfilm. The general answer from microfilm salespeople is usually: "No problem. Microfilm has been accepted as evidence and it is perfectly legal to microfilm. There is no cause for worry." I recommend that you do not take the issue so lightheartedly, however. Although it is true that microfilm is accepted in general as representing a true and authentic document, many regulations do not allow microfilm. For instance, the Occupational Safety and Health Administration does not allow microfilming for certain records, and various states do not allow microfilming for medical records during a certain period (2-15 years of activity) or many other applications. You have to check the legal requirements for your application very carefully before entering into a microfilm program.

There are three legal bases for evidence: (1) a statutory basis (an act such as the Uniform Photographic Act [UPA]); (2) common law ("best evidence" and "original document"); and (3) the business records exception to hearsay rule. One of the best resources on this issue is George Harmon's *Legality of Microfilm*, and a classic text to be consulted is a report prepared for Eastman Kodak, "Admissibility in Evidence of Microfilm Records."[1] The Internal Revenue Service has revoked its original opinion that microfilm reproductions of general books of accounts are not acceptable for purposes of determining tax liability.[2]

In most cases whether or not microfilm is legal depends on the microfilm process and its storage. One cannot say that microfilm is legal, only that certain forms of microfilm are legal if the proper procedure for filming has been used and if the microfilm is stored and preserved in the appropriate way.

In certain areas special care has to be taken regarding possible legal implications. One of them is updatable microfilm; the second is dry processing of microfilm. Others may depend on the application and local, state, or federal laws. The research into the legality of microfilm in your state, in your application, and in the way you are planning to produce and store the microfilm may be cumbersome, but it is certain to be challenging and rewarding. The National Micrographics Association (NMA) should also be contacted for assistance.[3]

In a recent survey, 78.6 percent of the microfilm users surveyed stated that their primary reason for using microfilm was "disposal of hard copy," followed by "security and protection of vital records" (73.2 percent), and "operating efficiency of active records" (66.7 percent).[4] In regard to savings to the company as a result of the microfilm program, 81 percent stated that there were savings, 9.5 percent saw no savings, and the remaining 9.5 percent did not know or did not respond to this question. Savings can be achieved if the appropriate system is selected and implemented in an efficient way.

The psychological and organizational wish to get rid of paper seems to be the main reason for going to a micrographics program. The need to keep information in a safe way seems to be another main reason for microfilming. With this consideration, it is more important to follow all recommendations for keeping an original microform and a working copy. It is always recommended to make a copy of microfilm and keep this copy (or the original) in a location that is safe, humidity and temperature controlled, and in conformity with the preservation requirements for microfilm.[5]

The records manager considering a conversion to microfilm faces a number of choices: which reduction ratio; what kind of microform; and which kind of retrieval system. When selecting a microfilm system he or she should consider the four essential decisions—format, indexing, environment, production rate—very carefully. On the basis of these decisions it becomes possible to make a proper selection of equipment and vendors.

Roll Film

Of the various types of microforms, roll film is the traditional form, providing low-cost production and high-speed retrieval, particularly when it is used in automated retrieval devices. Roll film applications include 35-, 16-, and sometimes 8-millimeter film. Reduction ratios range from 12:1 to 48:1. For archival purposes a lower reduction ratio should be chosen, from 12:1 to 18:1. Roll film applications are limited by one disadvantage, namely, the lack of economical means of updating the information and/or changing individual images.

A typical rollfilm application is office records that do not have to be updated individually, like records of checks, accounts ledgers, shipment and receipt records, and listings. Their retention period is in the medium range, and thus a higher reduction ratio can be taken, from 32:1 to 40:1.

Another typical roll film application is micropublishing, in which highly active listings and indexes are microfilmed and distributed on roll film. Subscribers to these publishing services can use high-speed readers that feed the roll film to the designated area from where the operator wants to retrieve information. Such information is never changed or updated by the user. If and when there are changes, the micropublisher distributes an updated roll or cartridge to the subscriber.

As we can see, roll film is best suited for applications in which the information has to be stored for legal or other reasons but is rarely changed or updated. Rarely is it acceptable for case activity or random activity, but it is ideal for information that has to be referenced very actively without actual changes. It is a typical "read only" application.

Roll film provides a high measure of file integrity. Information can be added *in sequence*, so that whole batches of documents can be filmed and added in sequence. Automated microfilm readers can be used for this application. They use various techniques to index the negative original from silver halide film.

Flashcards, odometer, image count, bar or code line, photo-optical code, and OCR (optical character recognition)[6] are technical methods for indexing individual images on the roll film and finding the one required in seconds. Such automatic search devices are connected to a microprocessor to provide computer-assisted retrieval (CAR).

Microfiche

With roll film thousands of images are dealt with as a unit. When information is inserted or updated, the total film of typically 2,500 images has to be changed or replaced. With this disadvantage of roll film in mind, one can see the need for smaller information units. Such are microfiches. Microfiches are card-size (4 by 6 inches, or 105 by 148.75 millimeters, almost A 6 size) unit records holding between 20 and 270 images. Ultrafiches with high impact density and maximum reduction can hold more than 1,000 images per fiche. The Bible has been reproduced on such a microfiche.

At a reduction ratio of 24:1, a fiche has 7 rows with 14 columns holding a total of 98 images per fiche. For COM applications a reduction ratio of 42:1 is used, providing 13 rows of 25 images each. This provides 325 images of letter-size images (8.5 inches by 11 inches). These COM microfiches are arranged so that the pagination sequence is in vertical columns across the fiche from left to right, whereas the normal sequence on fiches is left to right, top to bottom.

There are many systems advantages to having microfilm in card-size format, which allows filing in trays and cabinets like a conventional card filing arrangement. There are automated retrieval devices for microfiches on the market, among them System M from Access Corporation in Cincinnati, Ohio. These devices select the individual microfiche out of hundreds of thousands.

"Updatable" microfiches have been made available, too. However, the fact that images can be added or changed causes legal problems, as it may be difficult to prove the authenticity of records or documents.

Microfilm Jackets

This is the most flexible microfilm system. It is a sort of "microfilm folder" containing a number of images related to a case. Images can be added, or even rearranged, as required. The jackets are the same size as the microfiche. Automated machines cut and feed the film strips into the sleeves of jackets. Also, the transparent cover of the jacket protects the image and provides a longer life span. Of course, microfilm jackets are more expensive than roll film or microfiches. Therefore, jackets are only to be recommended if fiche or roll film is not acceptable to your application.

Aperture Cards

Any records manager who is in charge of storage of large drawings, like engineering drawings, knows that the size of the original drawings causes many problems in handling and storing. By converting such a drawing to a 35-millimeter format and mounting it on a tab-sized aperture card, you get a convenient carrier of this valuable drawing that can easily be indexed, sorted, and handled. For higher quality, 105-millimeter microfilm is used; it, too, can be blown back up to its original size and exposed on high-quality photographic paper. When this is developed, the copy is corrected, refilmed, and used for reprints of the updated information.

Computer Output Microfilm

Computer output is causing problems for records managers. A computer can produce a tremendous volume of information, which has to be recorded and handled. By printing such information on hard copy as computer printouts (CPOs) the records manager may end up with reams of printouts, which are difficult to handle and to store. Also, they tie up printers, and the recording of such information on paper is relatively expensive.

Computer output microfilm (COM) is a great help here, as it reduces bulk substantially. A 100-foot roll of 16-milimeter film may contain a maximum number of 2,000-3,300 images, depending on the format. A 3,000-page report, for instance, recorded in comic mode at 33 frames per foot (letter-size) will require less than the capacity of one 100-foot roll film. Can you imagine how much easier it is to distribute a roll of film rather than a 3,000-page report to users?

The second great advantage of COM is high speed. COM recorders are more than 10 times faster than line printers. This results in full use of computer capabilities that cannot be used with line printers. The third advantage is easy duplication. A microfiche containing 98 pages can be duplicated in 2-10 seconds, the time it takes to produce less than 10 paper copies. Because of these advantages COM is less expensive than paper copies.

One of the greatest advantages of COM is the ability to "digest" lots of information. With the right software, COM units can change virtually incomprehensible data tables into visuals capable of displaying a large amount of interrelated information. Listings of data may not mean much to the operator, particularly, if the listings are of heavy volume. Graphic images produced by COM have the capability of showing complex functions one against the other or in combination with an axis. A typical applications could be charts of sales or deviations from budgets, including many individual items.

Here is a comparison of paper copies and COM:[7]

	Paper Copies	COM
Number of pages	43,200	168 fiches
Stock cost	$180.00	$7.00
Shipping weight	480 pounds	2 pounds
Shipping cost	$200.00	$3.36
Printing time	5 hours	25 minutes

To create COM one can choose from four basic techniques: cathode ray tube (CRT); electron beam recording (EBR); (3) laser beam recording (LBR); and (4) fiber optics.

The oldest technique is CRT. An electron beam draws the desired characters on the face of the CRT. The image of the character then passes through a semireflective mirror-lens system on the unexposed film. After this, as the page is exposed to the film, the film is advanced, and the same process follows for the next page.

The EBR method writes the characters directly on the unexposed silver halide film. It can be developed by heat processing, not by wet processing. If a form slide is desired, its image is placed on the film using a second lens system, after the data is written on the film.

LBR also enables characters to be written directly on dry silver film, which is then processed by heat. A positive image is produced, in contrast to the negative original from silver halide film.

In the fiber optics technique a matrix of luminous fibers is selectively illuminated to form a line of characters. Then the film is exposed to the line of characters and incremented to permit the next line of characters to be generated. The forms overlay process is accomplished with a second lens system, as in the EBR process.[8]

IN-HOUSE MICROFILMING VERSUS CONTRACT FILMING

When considering microfilm we have to decide whether the filming should be done in house or by a contractor. In fact, this is a question we may want to pose regularly, after we have started microfilming. In-house filming means buying the equipment and do the filming, and sometimes even the processing ourselves; contract filming means that the filming and the processing is done by a microfilm company, usually a service bureau specializing in this kind of work. The decision depends on financial considerations, the level of control required, the logistics of distance and separate operation, the requirements for customizing, and operational considerations such as personnel availability, training and technical confidence, and the quality control system.

Under financial considerations we have to consider whether enough financial resources are available to operate an in-house microfilming section. Substantial capital is required to buy or lease equipment, including camera(s), reader/printer(s), and readers. As indicated in the section on cost management of microfilm in Chapter 3, in-house filming is often more expensive than contract filming. These service companies have specialized in this kind of work and so have more volume and easier means of quality control than does the normal record department.

In-house filming is attractive to organizations mainly because all records can be kept within the organization and there are tighter controls on the records while they are microfilmed and afterward. Management often has good reason to dislike a process that involves taking records out of the system. When records are taken out of the system to be sent to the microfilming company, the information is not available on short notice, and there is the possibility of a leak in confidentiality. By converting information onto microfilm in house, documents never leave the premises and are more secure and accessible. If outside microfilming is an ongoing operation, records have to be packed and shipped and care taken that records do not get out of sequence. An outside microfilm operation is beyond the records manager's control. Furthermore, the microfilming company may not treat your records in the special way they require. There is often little room for customizing in a commercial microfilming company.

For these reasons many records managers and their organizations prefer in-house filming, even though it may be more expensive. When considering in-house filming, careful analysis should be done as to the availability of personnel and the training and technical expertise required. It is important to have a good quality control system and a good inspection system and to watch out for the possible pitfalls mentioned above.

STORAGE OF MICROFILM

Microfilm storage depends on the microform used. Roll film and cartridges are stored in containers and trays, sometimes on specially designed shelves and cabinets. The most common format of microfilm is the fiche and the jacket, which can be stored in the work station, and in filing cabinets, open trays, frame stands, rotary cabinets, high-density shelving, and automated retrieval units (see Plates 4.1 and 4.2).

It is distressing to see how casually microfilm is stored in many record departments, sometimes in old cardboard boxes or similar containers. Care should be taken that equipment is used that has been designed and manu-

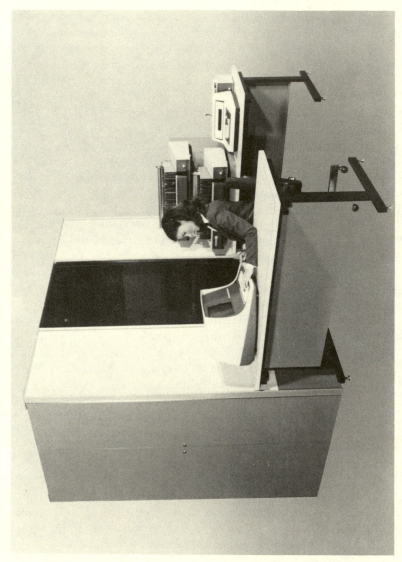

4.1 Automated microfilm retrieval system: System M holds 160,000 aperture cards or up to 100,000 fiches or jackets per module. It retrieves automatically in 6 to 20 seconds per retrieval. Courtesy Access Corporation.

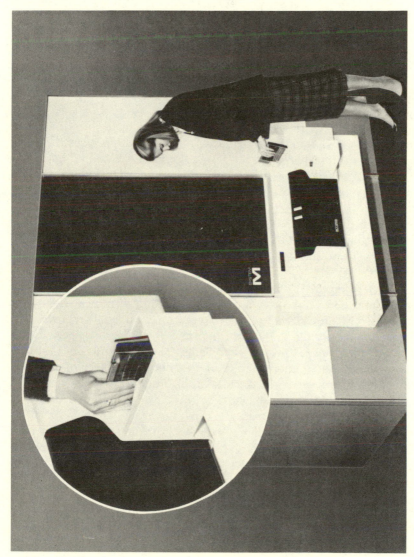

4.2 The automatic delivery system stacks pulled files in retrieved order. Courtesy Access Corporation.

factured for the purpose of microfilm storage. Such equipment, like Wilson Jones' Fiche Tray or Stor-Wel System's trays can store up to 1,200 fiches. Micro Design's Fiche Pocket can be attached to any surface and holds up to 50 fiches or jackets. Companies like RotaScan offer carousel-style units, Acme Visible Records, Inc., its Super Visible frames, and a range of companies sell specially designed cabinets for microfilm. Of course, any kind of manufacturer of four-by-six-inch card storage equipment that has been tested for microfilm storage can be chosen for storage of fiches and jackets. Microfilm's success as a storage media depends on the quality of filming, the material of the film, and the environment and conditions the microfilm is stored in. Particularly for long-term storage, a preservation policy should be established.

Does microfilm require a retention policy? Often we believe that once information is transferred to microfilm it will stay there forever and does not require any care. This belief can lead to disaster. Microfilm has to be taken care of, it has to be controlled under very strict and controlled conditions if we want to keep it long term. Such a preservation policy, as described later in this chapter, may be difficult to introduce. It may also be costly. Therefore, a records manager should design retention schedules for microfilm in the same way as for hard copy.

Short- and Medium-Term Storage

Short-term storage of microfilm covers storage up to three years from the date of filming. These records can be in roll film, fiche, cartridges, or jackets, all of which can be considered very safe. Medium-term storage, that is, up to seven or ten years from the time of filming, is generally still without any problems. However, there have been cases of records being damaged over a period of more than seven years because of lack of humidity control. Other users have reportedly lost the information on microfilm after spray-painting the microfilm cabinets. For storage of microfilm over five or seven years, care should be taken as to how the records are being kept.

Anyone storing records for more than seven to ten years should read carefully the following sections on long-term storage and the development of a conservation policy, parts of which will also apply to older records in medium-term storage.

Long-Term Storage

Unfortunately, many records managers have been led to believe that once information is put on microfilm it will *always* stay there. I have heard sales representatives of microfilm companies state openly, "I guarantee the life of microfilm for over 200 years." Such statements are irresponsible and false. Microfilm is very safe for short-term storage. Its safety record in regard to long-term storage, that is, in excess of ten years, has to be examined carefully. It depends on many factors, such as film, processing, storage conditions, and handling.

Microfilm is a very sensitive chemical product and can be influenced or damaged by a number of factors. There are six different kinds of damages that can befall microfilm: fading emulsion problems, blackouts; records becoming brittle and illegible; chemical separation of fluid; and fungus. When asked what causes these damages, one has to answer in general terms: chemicals, in the air and in the environment. Microfilm companies recognized this years ago when they recommended storing microfilm in long-term storage boxes, which were to be sealed and were supposed to protect microfilm from the damaging elements in the environment.

Today we know that neither closed steel nor plastic containers are good for long-term storage of microfilm.[9] Actually, instead of storing microfilm in any closed container, it is recommended to store microfilm in an environment where the air is steadily moving. One of the major factors the concerned records manager can easily improve is the room temperature and level of humidity in the area where microfilm is stored. Further factors are smoke and contact with paper and rubber bands.

At the time of this writing, there is very little concrete data available on the hazards of microfilm and their possible prevention. For long-term preservation of microfilm some experts suggest dry freezing, a process which is little understood and even less used by records managers. There is no track record on this process, and experts consider it an unproven preservation method. Anyone concerned with long-term storage of microfilm should take certain precautions, as listed in detail in the next section. The point is that it is irresponsible to put valuable information on microfilm and then not take care of it.

Certain microforms are better protected than others. Records managers choosing among roll film, cartridges, cassettes, fiches, jackets, and aperture cards should know that jackets are considered the safest form because the plastic protection of the sleeve delays possible damages. The mistake often made by records managers is believing microfilm to be a permanent and self-contained information carrier. Microfilm needs careful preservation under controlled conditions and therefore should also be subject to a retention policy.

PRESERVATION POLICY

When should one have a preservation policy for microfilm? Whenever microfilm is stored on a long-term basis, that is, more than ten years. If the information is very valuable, the records manager may implement part of this preservation policy if information is stored for more than seven years on microfilm. It is up to the records manager to decide whether to follow every recommendation or to select the parts that are feasible for the specific operation.

There are three areas of preservation: film and its preservation itself; making the environment clean for microfilm; and inspection and salvage of endangered information. Generally, the first step toward a preservation policy is to keep the original microfilm in a secure place that is protected from negative influences on the material. Only working copies should be used for working purposes, that is, for retrieval and at users' stations. In most cases these would be diazo copies of the original microfilm. The original microfilm is the document that is to be protected by being kept in an environmentally clean area. It should not come in contact with old nitrate film, water, cardboard, paper or similar items, or rubber bands.

Until 1950 nitrate film was often used for microfilming. Nitrate film more than any other film, however, disintegrates and therefore is no longer considered acceptable for microfilm. The sale of this kind of film was discontinued in 1951. If departments still have old nitrate film from before 1951, it should not be allowed to come in contact with newer films. Microfilm that is to be stored for ten years or more should be archival film. The records manager has to be very careful in selecting only high-quality film.

What is archival film and how can we make sure archival film is used in house or by a microfilm service company? The National Micrographics Association (NMA) and the federal government have firm standards for archival microfilm, which have to be observed. Most standards in this regard come from the American National Standards Institute (ANSI). For instance, only silver halide microfilm is acceptable for federal applications, meeting the requirements for Federal Standard No. 125 D, *Film, Photographic and Film, Photographic, Processed (for permanent records use)*; and the specifications for safety of photographic film, PH 1.25-1976 by the American National Standards Institute (ANSI) should be a requirement for any records manager. In addition, one should adhere to the requirements from the same institute, PH 1.28-1976, for silver gelatin-type film on cellulose ester base for archival records, and PH 1.41-1976 for photographic film for archival records, namely silver gelatin-type on polyester base.

Of course, processed microfilm should never be brought in contact with wter. If there should be a pipe breakage or the sprinkler system should go off and the microfilm gets wet, keep the microfilm in water or in wet condition and send it to a microfilm company as soon as possible. They can salvage it, or at least part of it. Drying microfilm after it has accidentally come in contact with water will create a chemical lump.

The American National Standards Institute has also specified standards for storing microfilm long term and/or permanently: PH 1.43-1976 requires roll film to be wound on cores of reels made of noncorroding materials such as nonferrous metals or inert plastics. Other metals may be used provided that they are safe. Coated metals that may exude fumes during storage may not be used.

Microfilm also should not be brought in contact with paper, cardboard, or any similar item. The acid in the paper influences microfilm and can damage it. There are a number of wallets on the market for storing microfiches such as paper envelopes. If they are coated with nondamaging material, then it may be all right to use them. The American National Standards Institute again specifies paper with regulation PH 1.53-1978. Reels of roll film are often shipped with cardboard cores. For long-term storage, it is recommended to take those cardboard cores out as soon as you receive them.

Rubber bands have chemicals in them that also damage microfilm if stored long term.

Reels of film (roll film, for instance) should be cleaned once a year or more frequently, depending on the activity. When storage in a safe is considered, the records manager should inquire about the safe's construction. A number of safes discharge a chemical foamlike substance when exposed to extreme heat. Many of these substances are very damaging to microfilm. Therefore, the records manager must check the safe's specifics before storing original microfilm in such a safe.

After ascertaining that microfilm will not come in contact with any of these damaging elements, the records manager should make sure that the environment is "clean." A clean environment is one in which the air temperature and humidity are controlled and the amount of pollutants is minimized. Most important is that the humidity be controlled in the area where microfilm is stored long term. The relative humidity of the storage area where microfilm is kept long term should not exceed 20-40 percent, with an optimum of 30 percent. Rapid and wide-range humidity changes should be avoided and not exceed a 5 percent change in a 24-hour period.[10] Secondly, the temperature should be controlled, not to exceed 70° F., or approximately 20° C. Rapid and wide-range temperature changes should be avoided, particularly any change over 5 percent in a 24-hour period. Color film should be stored at 35° F., or approximately 2° C.

Furthermore, certain pollutants have shown a damaging effect on microfilm, although very little is known about the level of pollution and the direct influence on microfilm. Reports have shown that smoking affects microfilm, as do fumes from photocopying machines, from certain cleaning materials, and particularly, from paint. Solid particles in the air, which may abrade the film or react to the image, should be removed by mechanical filters. Therefore, air cleaning devices should be installed in the area where microfilm is stored long term. Mechanical filters, which have a cleaning efficiency of not less than 85 percent, are preferable to the dry media type.

The air should not only be mostly free of pollutants but also should be moving, not standing still.[11] This is often done with a large fan in the microfilm area. In addition, gaseous impurities such as peroxides, oxidizing agents, sulphur dioxide, and hydrogen sulfide that cause damage or deterioration should be removed from the air. Archival microfilms should not be stored in the same room or in a room sharing the same ventilation as a room in which nonsilver gelatin films stored.

This may all sound confusing, but the records manager has a duty to give clear instructions in regard to the storage and handling of microfilm and its safety. Such safety measures include a cleaning process for roll film. Stand-alone cleaning machines, as available from Extek, will help to keep film clean and usable (see Plate 4.3).

But the real key to a good microfilm preservation policy is inspection. Depending on the condition of the microfilm area, there should be an inspection schedule based on number of years of storage. Inspection may have to be started after seven or ten years to make sure that any damaging process is discovered before the information is lost. When it is discovered that information is fading or becoming illegible, an attempt should be made to salvage or recover the information before it is finally lost.

The extent of damage found, the importance of the information, and the resources available will determine further actions in regard both to salvage attempts concerning the information recorded on the microform and to corrective measures in the preservation policy and its implementation. The first action may include a statement from the records manager as to why and how the information was lost and any reconstructive information available that can help recover the purpose and content of the original document. The second will describe the changes made in the preservation policy to avoid or minimize future incidents of information loss.

This inspection should be carried out every six months, every year, or every two years. As an example, Federal Regulations Nos. 101-11.507.2

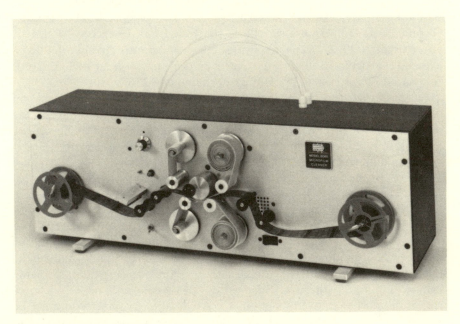

4.3   Stand-alone microfilm cleaning machine. Courtesy Extek, Inc.

require federal agencies to inspect the master film every two years of their scheduled life. The volume of images inspected depends on internal policies, on the value of information stored, and on the results of inspections of old films. For instance, this regulation requires inspection of 1 percent of all stored microfilms, randomly selected, of which 70 percent have not been tested previously, 20 percent have been tested in the previous inspection two years before, and the remaining 10 percent are from a fixed control group, representing the oldest and newest microfilm samples. Guidelines for such an inspection are provided in National Bureau of Standards Handbook No. 96, *Inspection of Processed Photographic Record Films for Aging Blemishes.*

In other organizations, microfilm inspection every five or seven years has been very successful. In this instance, a larger portion than 1 percent, usually 5-10 percent, is inspected. Should a record department find that a substantial part of such an inspection is showing negative results, action must be taken in regard to the microfilm's storage and preservation. An examination should be undertaken to detect possible reasons for damage or aging the film and a careful analysis made of storage conditions.

It should be mentioned at this point that the inspection process is a cumbersome activity. Employees should be assigned limited time spans for this activity, say 40 minutes or one hour at a time. After that activity the employee should be given a different activity, or time off to relax. Rotating employees is recommended. The records manager should also be aware that some unions and institutions are looking into the effects of microfilm reading on eyesight. At the time of this writing no final results have been published on this subject.

EQUIPMENT

Cameras and Recorders

Every microfilm program depends on the quality of the information's reproduction, which in turn depends on the equipment used to produce the microfilm itself. The selection of the microfilm camera is governed by the format of microfilm to be chosen, the quality necessary for the application, and the production rate required to make microfilming an economically justifiable venture.

The planetary camera, which has lamps built into the camera to provide controlled lighting and filming, was the traditional camera. These originally overhead photographing devices can produce only a single or double frame at a time, and since both the microfilm and the photographed material are stationary, the image quality produced is somewhat higher than the quality possible with a rotary camera. The trade-off for this better quality is lower speed than is possible with rotary cameras.

New developments have increased the speed of automated planetary cameras substantially. Cameras like the one from Bell & Howell offer good productivity with the traditional high quality of planetary filming (see Plate 4.4). Users report a satisfactory clarity of filmed material. In considering the records manager's attempts to get executives to use microfilm readers, we should not forget that the quality of film is the key factor in this struggle.

In the rotary camera filming process, paper and film move in unison, and the image is photographed via a series of mirrors through a slot device through which the paper passes. Rotary cameras are used primarily for large quantities of uniform-size sheets that require quick processing but not fine detail. You have to judge yourself what quality of image is both acceptable to your organization and economical. Most rotary models film on 16-millimeter stock, are easy to operate, have fast filming speed (for COM applications up to 20,000 exposures an hour), and are relatively inexpensive. For computer printout (CPO), a special camera is available with a larger opening to accept line printer printouts. Since 1975 rotary cameras have been equipped with built-in quality control, which has helped to assure the quality of the filming operation.

In both technologies, new cameras have been developed in recent years that speed up the operation, provide better quality, and often combine the filming process with the actual processing. Microprocessors are being used to monitor the filming operation, enhance operation, and increase productivity. Many cameras offer automatic feed of documents into the camera, which increases productivity substantially. Exposure controls automatically compensate for variations in the lighting intensity and the reflectivity of the materials filmed. Most microfilm managers do not have to worry about the three critical areas of microfilming—resolution, density, and contrast—because the new cameras with their latest technology monitor the filming process.

Readers

Readers are an important part of microfilming work operation, and they are among the most critical pieces of office equipment and/or office furniture. An unsatisfactory reader can cause employee problems, including low-morale. Quite often the reading operation is looked upon as the most unsatisfactory work task; operators of readers complain of eye strain and other health hazards, some of which are shared with operators of computer video display terminals. The records manager should check to see not only that the screen is large enough to take the full image of the largest forms ever used in the organization, but also that the illumination is sufficient. Clarity is a very important criterion when selecting microfilm readers. Also, the screen surface should be checked for glare. The location of the reader may have to be changed if there is any reflection from sunlight or any other bright light source. Various screens are available that reduce eye fatigue. However, it is the quality of microfilm, its clarity and brightness, that makes

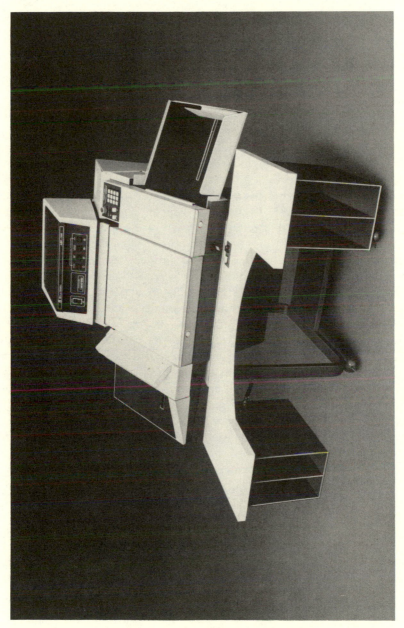

4.4   Planetary microfilm camera/recorder. Courtesy Bell & Howell.

the difference. Resistance to scratches and even distribution of illumination are features one should look for. The focus should be consistent. Check to see whether the image shifts its position on the screen when you operate the focus and whether the image stays in focus when you advance frames.

There is no question that the micrographics industry would be much more advanced had it developed a "magic way" to overcome the negative experience of working with a microfilm reader. Nevertheless, the reader is a necessary link in the micrographics process. Selection criteria for a reader are easy and comfortable operation, environment, microform system selected, users' need, and costs.

The range of readers available starts with hand-held readers. These are projection readers with simple, low-cost magnifiers, usually 10-12X, and are only good with 24X fiches.[12] Topper Micrographics offers the PLM-46 palm reader, a four-by-six-inch small-screen reader. Briefcase-size portable readers are available from Realist and Topper. These portable readers operate on self-contained batteries, electrical power sources, or automobile lighters.

Desktop units, the most common kind of readers, are offered in a wide range of magnifications. They have larger screens than portable readers, and, generally, illumination and film handling are better than with portable readers. At the top of the line are console model readers. These are very flexible in regard to handling different microforms, and some may even handle, or can be adapted to handle, multiple microforms. There is a need to make readers universal for different microforms, like cartridges, roll film, microfiches, and jackets. The reader industry has responded with more models that can handle the interchange through easy replacement of the film carrier.

When an application requires not only the "read only" feature of readers but also a fast and easy way of conversion to hard copy, the reader printer has its place. In addition to delivering an enlarged viewing image on the screen, it can produce paper copies of microfilmed documents. This is the convenient "retrieval machine for microfilm." Reader printers are available for all microfilm formats and range widely from manual to automatic film handling and operation. When selecting equipment, the records manager should look for easy loading and transporting of film, clear image capabilities, and good, steady focus.

Four different processes are used in the printing process: First is the silver process reader printer which uses the wet or dry silver process. In the wet silver process, a print can be produced in less than a minute (though it has to dry). The dry silver process is faster, but the paper darkens after a few months. For long-term or archival storage purposes, dry silver processes are not recommended. Second, the electrolytic reader printer provides prints from negative microforms and negative prints from positive microforms. Third, the electrostatic reader printer of which there are two kinds. One uses a xerographic transfer process by which a latent image is formed on a metal plate during exposure and developed by a toner. The other uses an electrofactual latent image on sensitized paper, which becomes hard copy. Fourth, the wet stabilization reader printer uses conventional wet processing without the fixer and wash process. The unused silver halide is not removed but stabilized, which means that it is less affected by light and heat.

LEGALITY OF MICROFILM

It is truly a nightmare for any records manager to think that microfilm may not be a legal document. Such fears usually dawn on us when the microfilm program has been established. Since George Harmon has dealt with these issues in a thorough way (see note 1) this topic will be explained only briefly.

Let me state that when the appropriate procedure and materials are being used for microfilming and care is being taken in compliance with storage requirements, then in most cases, microfilm can be regarded as a legal document; that is, it will be admitted as evidence in court. Since 1946, courts have become accustomed to microfilm evidence.

The legal question of originality can be raised with every medium. Information recorded on paper can be changed with correcting type or whiteout; information on magnetic carriers can also be changed. Records management, as the authority that guards the originality and authenticity of recorded information, is to take care that such recorded information is not altered. For these reasons, updatable microfilm loses the claim of authenticity and is usually not admitted as evidence.

There are three basic requirements for the preparation of microfilm as a legal document. First, the original record must be created in accordance with the professional requirements (quality of film, chemicals, resolution, etc.) and made in the regular course of business. Second, the microfilm must be stored properly and provide an accurate and durable medium for reproducing the original. Third, the microfilm record must provide satisfactory identification of the records. It is recommended that a written policy in the records department be prepared concerning microfilming of records, their storage, and identification.

NOTES

1. George Harmon, *Legality of Microfilm* (Chicago: Cohasset Associates, 1980); Nixon et al., "Admissibility in Evidence of Microfilm Records" (Rochester, N.Y.: Eastman Kodak, 1971).

2. Helen R. Harden, "Determining the Legality of Microfilm," *Information & Records Management* 12, no. 9 (September 1978): 86.

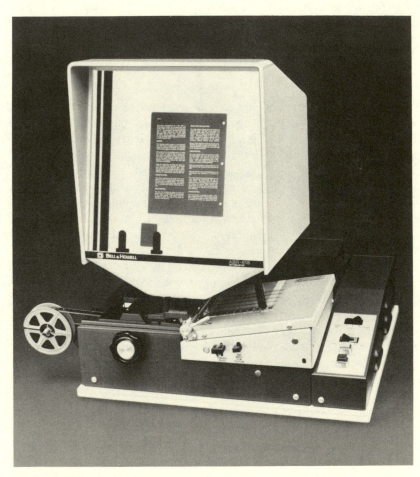

4.5 Reader/printer. Courtesy Bell & Howell.

3. See the listing of associations at the back of this book.

4. Milwaukee ARMA Chapter, Research Committee, "Your Micrographics Program," *ARMA Quarterly* (January 1982).

5. See the discussion of preservation policy later in this chapter.

6. See the description of OCR in Chapter 5.

7. Leonard S. Lee, "Information Management at the Crossroads," *ARMA Records Management Quarterly* 16, no. 2 (April 1982): 12.

8. Vinson Hudson, "Cost Effective Microform for Storage and Retrieval," *The Office* 93, no. 4 (April 1981): 82-83.

9. See *Storage and Preservation of Microfilm*, D-31 (Rochester, N.Y.: Eastman Kodak Company).

10. General Services Administration, National Archives and Records Services, Office of Records and Information Management, *Micrographics Systems Analysis*, Records Information Handbook, no. 7610-00-181-7579 (Washington, D.C.: U.S. Government Printing Office, 1974).

11. *Storage and Preservation of Microfilm*.

12. Ellen Mainiero, "Microfilm Readers and Reader Printers: State of the Art," *Information & Records Management* 16, no. 4 (April 1982): 30.

5

COMPUTERIZATION

WHAT COMPUTERS CAN DO FOR
RECORDS MANAGEMENT

Every records manager is steadily exposed to threats from the data processing department and/or the data processing profession. "Records management is outdated," we hear, "the future belongs to computers." "If a
records manager does not jump on the bandwagon of information systems
management fast, she or he will miss the boat." Chapter 6 will deal with this
issue as it affects the records manager professionally. For now, let's explore
what computers can do for the records department.

In most cases, the records manager does not have to worry about drastic
changes in archival storage of information for a few years. However,
certain changes will occur soon, perhaps at the very moment you read this.
These changes are increasing COM applications, spreading data processing
equipment, the expansion of word processing, and different requirements
for information handling, and these changes are affecting almost every
department. However, the field of records management will not be taken
over by computer technology as quickly as the areas of information
handling and processing. Information storage will probably be one of the
last areas data processing (DP) equipment will capture.

In the past, there were always experts to predict that records would soon
disappear, that the records management position would simply cease to
exist and new technologies would leave little or no space for old conventional record storage. I remember a meeting of top professionals in the field
of office technology in the late 1960s where a speaker said, "Well, folks, in
the 1980s we will not be dealing with paper, even at home. Then we will
have our coffee and doughnut in the morning and read the latest news on a

microfiche that we will be inserting into a microfilm reader on the kitchen counter. Those unhandy, heavy, expensive, and dirty newspapers will be eliminated by 1980.'' Well, it didn't happen and with some probability won't happen in the foreseeable future. However, there is no doubt in my mind that records will be stored on computer-usable media one day. The question is not if but when. In the meantime the records manager can make use of this technology and use it to manage associated processes such as indexing, word processing, record trace, retrieval assistance, and other statistical applications. While we are waiting for computer media to become more technically advanced for the storage of large volumes of information, we may as well use the computer to manage hard copy and microfilm.

Let us take a brief look at office automation in general and what can be expected in the next fifteen to twenty years. It is reasonable to expect that in the not too distant future the video display terminal will be the main information retrieval unit, providing stored and processed information of many different sorts. We shall be able to retrieve from the screen information displayed from the data processing network, records, information inputted by word processing, calculations, communications (within and outside the organization), image processing (graphics), documents in file, incoming and outgoing mail, telephone directories (personal, company, and other), information from every newspaper and periodical, full text, for the last century, all technical publications, calendars, tickler files, personal files, spelling dictionary, personal diary, time, and many other amenities.

At this point it may be useful to look at computerization in general, its myths, its advantages, and its disadvantages. When talking to many records managers who are approaching the question of whether to get a computer and, if so, which one, I first ask what they expect from computerization. In doing so, I have found that there are many myths about computers in circulation. So, let's have a hard look at the benefits of computers.

First, computers do not always "save people," that is, reduce the number of employees required to do a given job. Depending on the individual application, one should not automatically expect savings in manpower. After talking to hundreds of word processing users at seminars, I found personally that one-third of them used more people after they had installed a word processing system. The success of a system depends on how the system works, what kind of systems approach has been selected, and what kind of equipment has been chosen. Second, computers do not automatically save money. Again, the success depends on *how* it is done. The key to a successful computer system is a clear idea of objectives and criteria. Before we get involved in any computer program it is necessary to look at the present system, analyze its weaknesses, and look at the improvements a computer system should bring.

There is no point in staying away from computerization. When we use computers for managing individual tasks of records management with the help of data processors, we make our department more efficient and prepared for the future. Let's look at some of the applications.

The ideal computer system for records management is not available as a turnkey system (yet). Individual organizations have designed and implemented them, but nationwide there were only a few installed in 1982. A turnkey system would let the computer take care of the total records management program, starting with reference index, including a total file management program, with retention schedules for each record and a record-tracking program. Confidentiality issues can also be checked by the computer, that is, who is authorized to see a given record. Also, filing by activity can be managed more easily with the data provided by the computer on activity. Such complete records management programs are still expensive and out of reach for most records managers, though, so we will examine individual parts of such a program, which can be implemented in part as budget and circumstances allow.

Index

If an index is used to cross-reference from a name to a number or from one number or code to another, then this is the first application where records management should get actively involved in computerization. Unfortunately, there are hundreds of index systems developed and installed that do not work well or do not benefit the records manager. It is important to develop essential criteria and objectives that can be given to the data processing department, which should include a list of identifiers, that is, how the subject should be searched and identified. Next, the records manager has to decide whether the system should be on line or if it could be batch processing. Capacity is also quite often a problem. The computerized index should hold all names, numbers, and codes relating to the record system.

A very important objective is that the computer should select less than three index candidates from the total system. This means that out of the total volume, one, two, or three references are selected. Any screen selection that involves more than three references causes additional work to the operator, increases the error rate, and does not take full advantage of data processing capabilities. Quite a number of software programs do not select individual index candidates but rather display a full screen, or more, of names, numbers, or codes that have a common denominator. Then the operator has to select the appropriate name, number, or code of that listing. This leads to a high error rate because of the limited information displayed on the video display terminal (VDT, formerly CRT, or cathode ray tube). When establishing an index, it is best to program the computer, not the operator, to do the selecting. This is what the computer is there for.

Also, it is important to look in advance into the response time the computer system offers. Response time is the time period from the moment you ask for a reference to the time the answer is displayed on the screen. I have seen many systems that use software providing for a response time of up to 40 seconds. Systems with response time of 20 seconds and more are quite common. If your index is the main reference for the filing system and is used all the time, then you may want to make sure that you have a quick response time of not more than one second.

There is a great difference in file security between the old card index and a computerized index. Card indexes are always there. In some applications, the cards are stored in automatic rotary filing units, which break down on occasion. Then there is always the handcrank system, which cranks the required carrier to the posting board. Unless there is a major disaster, like fire, flooding, or earthquake, those index cards are always there. This is not so when you use data processing. Information can be lost during processing, and it can be lost from its files. Therefore, it is very important to have a good backup system, which should serve two purposes: provide you with the information when the processed volume is lost for some reason; and keep your department functioning while the system is operationally "down."

The backup index file should be stored in a safe place, usually away from the working copy. To make sure the file is protected against hazards that could damage the working index file, a different media is recommended. For handling purposes and for economics, many organizations are going to computer output microfilm (COM), which can be stored in a safe. However, check that the safe is "microfilm safe," that its chemical discharge is not damaging to microfilm. To be very safe, a records manager may prefer to store the backup index on hard copy, that is, on computer printout, which can be stored in a safe. A hard copy backup system is more expensive than COM and more difficult to handle because it entails reams of paper. If the backup system is provided on magnetic media, extreme care must be taken with regard to the storage of the record, which will be as vulnerable to damages from magnetic fields and static influences as its working copy.

When the records manager finally gets the computer index, she or he has to plan the conversion. All names, numbers, and codes have to be keyed into the computer, edited, and revised until the system works well. Depending on how much information is contained in the identifiers, it may take between one and three months for one person to key in every hundred thousand references. Experience has shown that the error rate on this kind of work averages 8 percent. This means that 8,000 of every 100,000 references have some kind of error that has to be corrected. One way to avoid such problems in the future is to put the reference cards in OCR format well in advance.

If you intend to get a computerized index in the future, you can start now to establish the identifiers and the information you will be using on the computer. You will have to start designing the system in conjunction with the data processing department, some consultant, or a computer company in advance. Once you have established the information base, you will generate each card with the same information you will be using with the computer. Each card is typed with identifiers and additional reference information. When it comes to conversion you can automatically scan the cards, speeding up the process drastically and avoiding input errors. This can be done in a local service bureau that has OCR scanning equipment, or you can buy a small, hand-held OCR scanner with the necessary hardware package. Remember that OCR works only with printed or typed information in this application. I recommend that you read carefully the section on data capture in this chapter.

In many cases it takes about a year to get the index in good working condition, so it is important to keep the old index as long as the system is being corrected and audited. If a system has substantial downtime or is on a batch-processing software package, a working copy of the index should be prepared, which may have to be on microfilm (roll film). This copy should be kept at the location where most of the inquiries for the index are handled. An automated retrieval device should be used in this case.

Let us take a look at typical performance objectives to be used when selecting, designing, or implementing an automated card index.

CRITERION ONE: THE CAPACITY OF THE INDEX MUST EQUAL THE TOTAL NUMBER OF PRESENT REFERENCES

To determine the capacity required, you will have to establish the total number of index cards to be converted. Partial conversion causes many problems and increases the error rate and therefore should not be considered. Count your present index to arrive at the total number of index cards to be converted, or even better, count one inch of your card index and multiply that number by the total inches of cards you have, to arrive at the total number of index items to be converted. An examination of your application and use of cards will tell you what expansion you have to add to your present index volume. It is usually true that you are required to keep the reference card only for as long as you keep the record. This means that the volume of your index is directly dependent on your retention policy.

CRITERION TWO: DETERMINE THE KIND AND NUMBER OF IDENTIFIERS AND THE NUMBER OF ACCESS POINTS

It is important for the records manager to select the right identifiers for the automated index. Identifiers are names, numbers, birth dates, addresses, or other specific description used for reference selection. With a card index you can add any information to identify the one John Jones you want, but with a computer index you have a predetermined number of characters with which to select the required reference. Therefore, it is important to select the identifiers that provide the best selection and require the least updating and the least memory capacity on the automated system.

It is also necessary to plan in advance the number of access points required. Access points are the areas of search within the index. For instance, an index providing cross-reference between names and numbers may require three or four access points if there are more than 500,000 names in the system. Then there are too many similar names or references with the same name to make the index workable. A second search field, like the birth date, may help to find the right reference; a third reference may be the home zip code. Additional access points mean in this case that the operator can search not only by name but also by birth date and zip code to identify the appropriate reference. The number of access points depends on the volume of the index and the cross-reference system itself.

CRITERION THREE: IF AN ALPHABETICAL INDEX IS INVOLVED, INCLUDE A SOUNDEX SYSTEM

A Soundex software program, readily available for most software packages, will identify names that are spelled differently but sound similar. This can be a great help. Also, automatic search by initial and first name comparable are very useful. With this feature you will not have to key in all demographic information twice. The system will search for the name under initial, first name, and comparable (R., or Robert, or Bob).

Measurable performance objectives are very useful, as they provide guidelines for measurable efficiency. If the reference system is used at different stations, the possibility of retrieving such information from the VDT should provide real savings and eliminate much internal communication (telephoning). In this case an objective would be to reduce such internal communication by a certain percentage. The higher the percentage achieved the better. Three other objectives are to decrease (or eliminate) time, efforts, and personnel expended operating the conventional card index by a certain percentage; to provide the selected reference from the total reference volume in one second or less (not to have a listing of possible references from which the operator has to select the appropriate one; and to gain a decrease in monitoring work of a certain percentage or number of man-hours).

Word Processing

Word processing (WP) can truly be called the fastest growing phenomenon in the office environment since photocopying. Word processing is the use of computer capability for creating, sorting, formatting, processing, and handling written communications. It is a very exciting concept that will revolutionize most standard office functions. Many records managers are already involved in WP. This section will examine the systems available, selection criteria, and implementation guidelines for WP.

The first question is, of course, when do you need WP? You may be able to justify WP under various circumstances:

1. When you have one or more people dedicated to typing on a daily basis, that is, heavy typing volume.

2. When you are producing long documents on a regular basis that require heavy proofreading and editing.

3. When your work process involves a drafting process before the final document is typed. In such cases executives like to see the drafted typed document, then make corrections, and request retyping.

4. When producing heavily formatted documents and reports on a regular basis.

5. When generating mass mailings.

6. When the image of the typed document is very important, such as in prospect letters for sales purposes.

7. When you are frequently producing repetitive letters with few changes.

8. When you are frequently revising existing reports.

9. When it is possible to use stock paragraphs and phrases in frequently generated documents.

If any of these conditions apply to your organization, you may be able to justify WP. Word processing is a wide field, and equipment costs range from $3,000 to well over $100,000. Before we start looking at design and selection of WP systems, we have to analyze the existing system, how it can be improved, and the criteria for improvement. The success of the implementation of WP equipment depends on the establishment of performance objectives and selection criteria, choosing the appropriate equipment category, and selecting the appropriate vendor and equipment. WP involves a wide range of individual systems, starting with "intelligent typewriters" and ending with small computer systems.

Records managers must examine carefully the level of computer capability required for a specific application. The two mistakes made in selecting word processing systems are "overbuying" and "underbuying." Overbuying is buying a word processing unit that has data processing power and memory that are not needed and will never be used. The system may be too complicated because of excessive features for a particular application. Of course, overbuying is uneconomical as too much money is spent on features and capabilities not helpful to the operator of a specific task. The second mistake is underbuying, that is, buying a word processing unit that is too small and does not meet the requirements of the particular job.

Eight different categories of WP units are available: electronic or "memory" typewriters; "blind" text editors; display text editors; multifunctional intelligent devices; shared logic text editors; distributed logic text editors; time-shared text editors; and integrated office systems.

The smallest kind of WP is the electronic or memory typewriter. These are single element typewriters (ball or print wheel) with some basic programming capabilities for easy correction. When editing features are available they are very basic. The IBM Selectric III is a good example of this type of equipment. Users with heavy typing, very little correction, and a low requirement for quality image love these machines for their reliability and simplicity. They are priced under $2,000, which makes them a reliable, economic workhorse. Particularly for transcription work for internal documentation (as required in medical applications, for instance), it is hard to beat the economics of these machines with more sophisticated WP equipment.

Blind text editors have more data processing power. This is usually translated into more memory and more editing features. As the name says, they do not have a display, be it a window for a line or a larger screen. However, their work capacity is equal to some text editors with display. If you own a good electronic typewriter you can buy the computer capability and a screen to connect to your existing typewriter. This way you can design your own display text editor without having to pay for a total new system.

The above categories have the added advantage that all the negative effects of work stations with video display do not apply. The section later in this chapter on terminals explains the stress and health hazards of VDTs and the recommendations for additional breaks during work and environmental conditions to be established for a VDT work station. None of these need be considered with the electronic typewriter or blind text editor.

Display text editors—also called dedicated word processors—consist of three elements: the keyboard; the display; and the typing or printing device. Some units combine all three functions in one piece of equipment; others combine the keyboard with a display "line," but most of the equipment in this category has a video display terminal (VDT). The display itself can be a string of characters, such as a partial line display of up to 20 characters or a line (linear display), which still may display only 32-40 characters. The more common display is on a screen, showing a partial or a full page. The partial page may have between 14 and 24 lines on the screen, and the operator has to "scroll" the text up or down to get the full document in view. Full-page displays offer the operator the full exposure of about 65 lines with 80 characters per line. In this case the characters and letters are sometimes smaller than on the partial display.

Multifunctional intelligent devices are WP/DP hybrids. In reality they are small computers that have been designed for a variety of functions, WP being only one of them. They can be used as a versatile information capturing and processing machine.

All the abovementioned WP categories use equipment on a stand-alone basis. The other four groups are interactive systems, using work stations connected to one or more central processing units (CPUs). These are shared logic text editors, distributed logic text editors, time-shared text editors, and integrated office work station systems. They will not fall within the records manager's decision field, as they are usually part of data processing's overall planning for your organization.

One of the key selection criteria for WP equipment is whether it can process simultaneously. Can you, for instance, edit while you are printing out, or do you have to wait until the printing function is completed, then edit, and then print?

In trying to avoid overbuying you have to take a hard look at the editing features the WP equipment offers. Do you need to handle a lot of statistics? Do you have to type onto many forms? Do you need the cursor to move in four positions (left, right, up, and down), or are two directions sufficient (left and right)? Will you be searching on a regular basis for certain words throughout the document? What search capabilities are required? Do you need to delete by document, page, paragraph, sentence, line, word, character, and block? Or would it be sufficient for the planned operation to be able to delete by document, page, paragraph, string of characters, word, and character? What hyphenation is required? Hot zone and scanning procedures, the most common methods, still require the operator's help. Hyphenation by formula or dictionary is much more complicated and expensive but does not require the operator's help. What arithmetic capability is required?

Then there are the equipment-related questions: What kind of media are used? Tapes, diskettes, minidisks, or cartridges? What media are used in departments that have to interface with the new system? Can you take the floppy disks from the system and use them in the equipment of another department? How much memory is required for this work station (1) on line and (2) off line? The average disk storage of 300,000 characters may translate into 60-100 pages. Capacities depend on the chip market. Presently, the most common capacities of on-line memory are 64, 128, and 256K (kilobytes). Be aware of the difference between ROM (read only memory) and RAM (random access memory). What programmable vendor-developed system is available? What other application packages can be obtained? Can the system be upgraded? Can OCR equipment be used? What speed of printer is needed? Does the offered equipment offer the best in work conditions and environmental requirements spelled out in the section below on data processing equipment?

Then there are questions about the designated operators for WP and their training, pay scale, job description, selection process, and so forth. During the training period only 40-90 percent of the planned productivity is achieved. For the purpose of measuring the performance of WP, you should not expect to achieve full capacity until 12 weeks to one year after installation. This factor should be included in the advance cost comparison between the existing system and a proposed WP system.

Word processing should be taken as one of the means of recording, handling, and processing information. The traditional function of records management lay only at the end of that process of information handling, namely, the storage of recorded information. Now we may want to look at the other end, the generation, creation, and recording of information. As far as new information is created in the form of documents of correspondence, the word processor will bring new methods. But when we want to include information that is already printed or typed, there are different technologies. The most promising of these technologies is optical character recognition, whereby a scanning device linked to a computer "reads" the typed or printed matter and feeds it into the computer, with fewer errors and much greater speed than any human could attain "keying in" such information.

Record Control Systems

There is no comprehensive computer available as a turnkey system which satisfies all the needs of records management. Also, it is not yet possible to store large quantities of data on computers economically. When we consider these facts we may wonder if there is not at least a technology to monitor and manage files with a little help from the computer. If record management's demand of our time is to use the computer to control hard copy, then it applies best to record control systems. Controls can be established with the help of a computer to check on authorization of access to records, to control the movements of records, and to control the length of stay at any location. Such systems are used for record control outside of the file room but within the same organization. In most cases they are used to control records within a building or among a number of individual users. Many record departments have manual systems to trace and monitor records' movements. They consist usually of books or ledgers in which records are logged in or out. There are three objectives of computer systems in this area.

The first is to eliminate manual writing and replace it with an easy procedure for logging in and out. The control process should also have means of detecting possible noncooperation of departments and/or individuals. The success of any record trace system depends on the way individuals will be forced to use the control procedures properly by virtue of the procedure's nature. If records are sent out to a department and this department does not log the record in, all computer power is useless in tracking down that record. Therefore, record trace systems should have means to overcome this liability. The second objective is to control individual movements of records and, if desired, link them to time spans, and the third is to make records immediately available by establishing the location of that information base at any time and therefore to retrieve or add information in case of emergency.

The advantages of these systems are obvious. They eliminate telephoning or chasing down records. They improve the efficiency and the external image of the organization by making it possible to locate records that have been sent to different departments almost instantaneously in response to long-distance telephone calls and similar information request. They also reduce activity in the records department as there is no need to go to the record room and search for a record, only to find that the record has been logged out to another department. The VDT will tell the inquirer that a record is not on the shelf in the record room but has been sent to department A, which received it at 3:30 P.M. If there is an emergency, this requester may be able to get direct help from department A, where the record is presently kept. Record trace systems can also mean personnel savings and savings in internal communications between users of records and the record department. Record systems can be more decentralized as there is full control over the information.

The equipment needed for such a system starts, of course, with a central processing unit (which could even be a microprocessor), a printer, and a number of terminals with/or without scanning devices for logging operations. The key to a smooth operation is a computer-readable identifier on the record itself. This should be in bar code or OCR format. OCR technology seems to be winning more acceptance because it can be read not only by computer but also by the human eye. Once all records are coded in printing or by label with a computer-readable index, the first requirement for record tracing is fulfilled as a computer can be used to read and monitor records.

The next step is to design and implement the computerized record tracking system. First, we have to establish an index on the computer. Second, we have to determine which control stations we want to use and how many. Record trace systems can be used to control 1 station or 1,250 stations. In the case of the single station the records manager wants to control the flow of records out of the file room. In most cases, however, individual departments, buildings, desks, or operational sections are used as control points. The operational need and the organization's structure (and, of course, the budget) will determine the number of control stations within an organization. Now we require a software package that deals with the volume of movements and either determines a movement as two actions (in *and* out) or provides a time limit on each user station. This is needed to make sure that users have to log the records in (acknowledgment that the record has arrived at this particular station). For instance, if the system is designed around the two-action movement idea, then the computer will detect that a record has been logged out and sent to department A. Let's assume department A has not logged it in. The computer will detect in this case the incomplete movement and indicate or print out that there is an incomplete movement. A record has been sent to department A that either did not get there or was not logged in. The subsequent inquiry to department A will discipline the people in that department after an initial period to make sure all records received are logged in. Otherwise they have to answer an inquiry from the computer or the record department, depending on the design of the system. The advantage for the records manager is that when there is a request that has been sent out, file clerks do not have to search in log books, on the shelf, or anywhere else for the record because the computer will not accept a retrieval request from the file room. Everyone can see at the terminals that the record was sent at a certain time to department C. If there is an emergency, the requesting user can request the record directly from department C, and when it is sent to the requester, the system again will keep track of it.

Such a system can be used for file folders, hard copy records of any size, computer tapes, disk packs, disks, X-ray film jackets, microfilm, or any combination of media. Each system can be designed to meet the company's or organization's needs. There could be just one control station to check on records leaving the centralized record room or literally hundreds of them controlling buildings, departments, offices, or desks.

Sometimes the main frame computer is used and a record control system is integrated into the institution's data processing center. Most of the major data processing companies can accommodate such a program; however, some companies have specialized in this field. Ames Color File Corporation was among the first to introduce that idea to the public, but it never achieved the development of a complete, stand-alone record trace system. At the time of this writing, Ames is selling bar code terminals without any software or hardware for the processing tasks. The company concentrates in this field on data capture only. The terminals have two-way communication possibilities.

TAB Products offers its System 7000, an electronic charge-out system. It does not, at the time of this writing, include a scanning device, but requires keyboard operation.

Datafile Ltd., a Canadian company with a subsidiary in Minneapolis, has developed a complete stand-alone system called Frolic (file room on line information control), which uses OCR technology. The system does not work on two-action movement control but on time control. Its software package is comprehensive and flexible. Datafile is, of course, known for its advanced method of color coding. At one of the company's first installations, a hospital in Florida, the system controls the movement of over 110,000 file folders to over 1,200 doctors with some 45 control terminals. At another installation, also in a hospital but in Chicago, 155,000 medical records are controlled by 34 VDT control stations. In Edmonton, Canada, the Department of Energy and Natural Resources of the Province of Alberta controls the movement of some 240,000 "land files," consisting of "surface files" and "subsurface files," with 40 control stations.

Another company specializing in this field is International Computing, now Contel Information Systems. They market a record trace system called the automated folder control system (AFCS). The Railroad Retirement Board received a record trace system to control some 2.5 million file folders. Contel Information Systems installed a minicomputer system to track folder movement by reading bar-coded labels on the folders.

Record trace is a viable computer application that will be quite common in the future. Records managers can prepare themselves for this task by designing in advance folders with computer-readable code, either in OCR or in bar code. When the time for the implementation of the record trace system comes, a good part of the records will then be prepared for the new system.

EQUIPMENT SELECTION

A major change is happening in the computer world. Companies and organizations are looking increasingly at the user friendliness of computer equipment. As computer equipment is installed in large quantities throughout the country, management becomes increasingly aware of possible health hazards, of ergonomics regarding work places, and acceptance of equipment by employees. The success of a new computer system is very much dependent on the acceptance of employees within the department. To overcome the resistance of individuals, the computer industry is working on equipment with better styles and more orientation toward the operator.

It can be generally said that in the past only computer experts were involved in selecting equipment. This is changing. Records managers should familiarize themselves with the differences in computer equipment and participate in the selection in regard to user friendliness. Let us compare the purchase of a computer system with the purchase of an automobile. Would you choose a car just by its engine power? Is it not equally important to check the seating arrangement, the dashboard, the overall style? The same considerations apply to the purchase of computer equipment. The style of the video display terminal, in front of which the operator has to sit for a full working day, may become as important as the style of a piece of furniture in the home. These illustrations are meant to draw the record manager's attention to the issue of user friendliness.

Processing Units

The Processing Unit (PU) is the heart of any computer. It houses the main processing device and the memory. In most cases, PUs are in the domain of the data processing department. The average records manager has little input regarding the choice or power of the processing unit. However, as minicomputers and microcomputers become more powerful and are used increasingly on a stand-alone basis, records managers have to deal with computer capacities.

Microcomputers are based on standard chips. Capacities are stated in terms of 32, 64, 128, or 256 K. The latest development, 256 K, gives eight times more storage capacity on-line as a 32 K unit. You will find that the memory is stated in read-only-memory (ROM) and random-access-memory (RAM). The latter is memory the operator can program and use to the need of the application. ROM is preprogrammed memory the operator cannot change. ROM is comparable to a device which has been programmed for certain functions before it was sold, while RAM is open to the purchaser's instructions.

Printers

Printers are the necessary type of output for most computers. First, before installing a printer, a records manager should select carefully a location for the printer which is easily accessible, but does not make the working conditions around the printer unbearable. Printers are by nature very noisy machines. To have to work all day next to a busy printer is one of the classic punishments of our time! A place should be found where the noise level of the printer can be tolerated. Also, it is recommended to buy in advance the best noise reduction equipment you can get. Hoods have been designed to quiet printers and they are well worth the money.

The speed of the printer and its reliability to the print and feed mechanism should be checked. Individual requirements depend on the department's application.

Terminals

When selecting a computer system, much care should be taken in regard to terminals. Terminals, once CRTs (cathode ray tubes), now known as VDTs (video display terminals), are very important for the success of any system. Some computer systems have been considered a failure not because of software or hardware trouble, but because of employee opposition to the terminals. VDTs are environmental furniture with which employees have to work constantly. Such terminals are a more vital part of the operator's working environment than any other piece of office furniture except the chair and the desk.

A number of factors are very important when selecting VDTs: color of screen and characters; design of keyboard; location of screen; overall design; and environmental issues. When selecting and/or implementing video display terminals, the records manager should be aware of VDTs' effects on operators who work at terminals most of their working day. First, there is the stress factor for a person working for longer time periods in front of the VDT. The National Institute for Occupational Safety and Health has issued a number of guidelines in its 1981 study, *Potential Health Hazards of Video Display Terminals.* Here are some of them:

1. The ideal lighting level for VDT operation is about one-third to one-half of that for reading hard copy. As terminal operators are likely to use both VDT screen and hard copy, NIOSH recommends a compromise level roughly midway between the optimum VDT level (one-third of reading level) and hard copy lighting level (15% light reduction).

2. Glare on the screen should be reduced. NIOSH suggests avoiding highly reflective surfaces, using screen hoods, antiglare filters, and direct lighting, and keeping shades and blinds drawn, particularly when the sun is shining directly through windows. It also recommends positioning terminals so that potential sources of glare are not located directly behind or in front of the screen.

3. Keyboards should have an adjustable height (H in Fig. 5.1) of 720-790 millimeters (approximately 28.5-31 inches). The work station should have enough leg clearance for operators.

4. Screen height and position should be adjustable to individual user preferences. The top line on the screen should fall just below eye level of a comfortably seated operator.

5. Screen center should be angled between 10 and 20 degrees below the horizontal plane at the operator's eye level (angle A in Fig. 5.1).

6. The distance between the eyes and the screen (C in the figure) should be 17.75-19.75 inches (450-500 millimeters).

7. The operator's chair should have adjustable seat and back heights and lower back supports.

8. Operators with moderate workloads should take a 15-minute break after two hours of continuous VDT work to relieve stress, monotony, and eyestrain. For operators with heavy or highly repetitive workloads, the breaks should be increased to 15 minutes after every hour of continuous VDT work.

9. VDTs should not be operated by persons having uncorrected vision problems. NIOSH suggests preplacement vision tests for VDT operators.

In addition, operators should not wear bifocal glasses when operating a VDT for a longer time (see Plate 5.1).

But the main concern for any records manager and/or supervisor of VDT operators is potential health hazards for the VDT operator. Terminals have

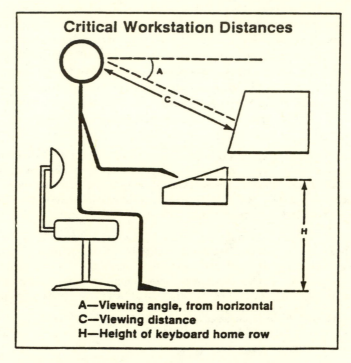

Critical Workstation Distances

A—Viewing angle, from horizontal
C—Viewing distance
H—Height of keyboard home row

5.1   VDT operator: distances for the work station. Courtesy IMRE.
          IMRE.

been blamed for a variety of illnesses and medical problems, ranging from eyestrain to miscarriage, from headaches to gastritis. At the request of labor unions, NIOSH studied VDT operators in 1981 and found that claims sometimes seem exaggerated but do have a real basis. In 1982, Boston University found that pregnant women were endangered working at VDTs. Warnings to that effect were reported repeatedly on the university's public radio station, WBUR, in Boston. Although NIOSH concluded that VDTs do not discharge harmful radiation or noxious fumes, as of now there is little hard data available about the low-level radiation of VDTs and their effects on operators, particularly pregnant women. Accepted is the fact that VDT operation is a particularly demanding line of work, more likely than other office tasks to produce tension-related illness, eyestrain, and muscle fatigue.

Because of above problems the records manager should be very careful regarding the selection of VDTs. The screen itself should be large enough to show a full page. (The characters may be smaller than with a half-page screen, but the advantage of a fully visible page is worth it.) If possible, a black and white screen should be avoided. Ideal is an amber background with yellow characters; however, you will not find too many vendors offering such systems. A green screen, that is, light green characters on a dark green background, is usually the compromise. Good results have also been reported from green characters on a charcoal-colored background. As recommended by NIOSH, the screen should be angled and should be non-glaring. Most VDTs allow the operator to adjust the brightness of the screen to the level of lighting and personal convenience. Screens that can be tilted and turned can be positioned to suit individual operators' requirements for a rotating operator work schedule. Also, the keyboard should be detached from the screen and flexible for individual arrangement.

The introduction of VDTs is such a tremendous change to employees that the psychological effects should not be forgotten. It is a good idea to have a selection of VDTs under consideration delivered to the office "on loan and dry," that is, unconnected and just for familiarization. Future VDT operators have a chance to select the design they like best. Having been involved in the selection process they will feel less alienated with the new equipment and accept the necessary work changes more easily.

Data Capture

Records managers may get more involved with the issue of information recording. The traditional role of records management focused on the last pieces of the chain of information handling, that is, storing information on records after the records had been created. However, the revolution in information management caused by different technologies may require records managers to get involved in the field of records creation, that is, in recording information. Recording information means making information permanent by writing it on paper, recording it on microfilm or computer media, even recording it on tape by dictating. We have discussed the issue of recording information on microfilm in Chapter 4. Recording of information on computer media or feeding into a computer may be a field records managers have to manage in the future.

Instead of keying information into the computer, devices can be used so that information can be scanned. Bar code technology is one of the means to capture a string of characters by moving a scanning device over the special code. This technology is limited in its overall scope because it requires a special bar code printer to attach or print the bar code to the document or package that you want to scan automatically. Such bar codes are standard on food packages and other items where the same information has to be captured over and over again.

More flexible and common is the optical character recognition (OCR) technique, whereby scanning devices can read most typed styles of letters and numbers (see Plate 5.2). There are two styles, OCR-A and OCR-B, but

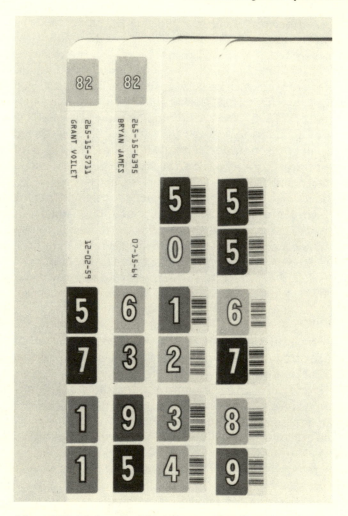

5.2   OCR label on file folder. Courtesy Datafile Ltd.

many scanners can read both styles. Most OCR readers can read typefaces like prestige, elite, courier 72, letter gothic, prestige pica, courier 12, pica 72, elite 72, advocate, delegate, and adjutant—basically any typeface produced on any typewriter. Depending on the device, scanners can read from 900 words per minute to 70-120 documents per minute on a continuous application. For word processing applications a speed of 50-240 characters per second can be achieved. Besides the technical advantages of such equipment, one should consider the immense accuracy possible with these scanning devices, from 98 percent to 99.9 percent, depending on equipment and process.

INFORMATION CARRIERS

Let us look at devices carrying information processed by the computer and produced as an output of any information processing. Paper is one of these carriers in the form of computer printout (CPO).

Printout Binders

Burst or unburst computer printout documents are stored in special document containers (see Plate 5.3). Some systems offered are hanging, others are standing laterally on shelves. These printout binders are available in standard printout sizes. The hanging type, comparable to lateral suspended filing, offers advantages in easy handling and accessing. Of course, printout storage has the same guidelines as paper storage, except that the sizes of printout may require special cabinets or housings.

Microfilm is the next medium in the form of computer output microfilm (COM). The transfer of information from microfilm into the computer is called computer input microfilm (CIM). However, most of the computer-related media are magnetic media. When storing magnetic information carriers we have to establish a specially protected environment. Not unlike microfilm, magnetic media require an environmentally controlled and monitored storage area. It is necessary to be aware of the possible environmental hazards: dust and accumulating dirt; static from electricity; magnetic influence; and temperature range.

Information is stored on magnetic carriers with high density. This density increases every year, making it possible for the computer industry to be more economical. But information stored in such dense places can mean disaster if dust or dirt affects the data capture. A records manager has to store magnetic media in very clean conditions. Even the air should be cleaned regularly. Magnetic storage media should be encased whenever possible.

Also, such media should not be exposed to static in a storage room. Precautions should start with selecting nonstatic carpeting and furnishings. A humidifier should keep the humidity at appropriate levels to avoid excess static. Power sources and power systems should be checked in regard to their location and their influence on the magnetic media storage system. Users have reported incidents of information erased and/or distorted by a power backup system within the same building or by influence from a building's power source. Finally, no magnets should be used near the area. There have been reports of magnetic watches damaging information on such media as tapes and floppy disks. Some office equipment requires magnets for operation and should not be used or stored in the same room where magnetic media are stored.

5.3   CPO storage unit. Courtesy Supreme Equipment and Systems Corp.

Let us look at the individual forms of magnetic media. In the group of small magnetic media we are dealing with the tape cassette, the data cartridge, diskettes (usually called floppy disks), the flippy disk (both sides usable), the Winchester disk, and minidisks.

Tapes

Magnetic tapes are best stored upright, hanging or standing. For storage and retrieval reasons hanging is the most common kind of storage of tapes (see Plate 5.4). Data tape cassettes are the same size as common tape cassettes, but data cartridges use quarter-inch instead of half-inch tape. The cartridge itself is a four-by-six-inch plastic housing. When tapes loosen up, they should be cleaned and tightened. A protective case is always preferable. Some companies provide color-coded indexing for tapes, as for file folders. This method of indexing eliminates misfiling and speeds up filing and retrieval time.

Diskettes and Disk Packs

The most common kind of magnetic storage equipment is the flexible diskette, or floppy disk. The diskette is a thin, disklike piece of magnetically coated plastic resembling a 45 rpm record. Diskettes are stored increasingly in decentralized places—close to word processors, microprocessors, or other stand-alone units. The records manager should make various departments aware of the potential hazards described above for other magnetic media.

Diskettes should always be stored in a special envelope with the processing slots down. They should not be bent. The temperature should never be below 50° F. or 10° C. There is also an upper limit of 125° F. or 52° C. I assume that very few records managers have working conditions with temperatures exceeding these!

The diskette has more storage capacity per unit than most other flexible magnetic media. It can hold between 80 and 150 double-spaced pages of text per side. The storage capacity varies by factors of backup index and whether it is single-sided or double-sided, single-density or double-density.

A minidiskette has a 5.5-inch diameter rather than the 7.5-inch dimension of a standard diskette. Overall storage capacity is about half of that of a regular diskette.

Winchester disks, available in four sizes, offer more capacity than regular diskettes, but have to be maintained in a contained environment, that is, as fixed on-line storage media.

Diskettes are contained in a nonremovable protective envelope (not to be mistaken for the storage envelope which is removed when the diskette is inserted into the drive) that shields the disk surface from contamination by dust, fingerprints, and other damaging factors. This protective cover has a

5.4   Lateral tape storage. Courtesy Supreme Equipment and Systems Corp.

round opening in the center and a long slot from the center toward the edge of the disk. This is the exposed part of the diskette where actual contact between the read/write head and the disk is made. This slot opening is to be protected carefully, and care should be taken that it is not touched. Here are the *do*s and *don't*s for diskettes:[1]

Do

Do be careful when inserting or removing the diskette from the disk drive.

Do keep the diskette in the plastic jacket when not in disk drive.

Do handle diskettes only by plastic jacket.

Do store diskette standing on its edge, or in specially designed diskette container or rack.

Do *only* use labels manufactured for use with diskettes.

Do index labels before placing them on diskette.

Do keep the disk drive clean, particularly the metal hub, to avoid buildup of diskette-damaging debris.

Do Not

Do not touch exposed areas of diskette.

Do not write on diskette surface.

Do not use erasers on diskette surface.

Do not attach rubber bands or paper clips to diskettes.

Do not place heavy objects on top of diskette.

Do not smoke, eat, or drink near diskette.

Do not stack diskettes on top of each other.

Do not place magnets near diskette.

Do not place diskette in direct sunlight or near direct source of heat.

Do not place diskette near motors, transformers, or power cords.

Do not place chemicals or cleaning solvents near diskette.

Do not place diskette where it could be exposed to water or any kind of fluid. Very little is known of the long-term effects of storage on magnetic media. The industry is new, and manufacturing processes have changed. We have to wait for information on long-term storage.

Disk packs, which contain a multiple of the information stored on disks, should be stored under the same conditions of controlled environment. Cabinets and housings are available, specially designed for safe storage of disk packs.

Video Disks and Optical Disks

The new disks are completely different. Video disks store information analog, television-type images on a frame by frame basis. Very few specialists believe at the time of this writing that video disks will have a major impact on records management. The call for the future is for a record storage medium which can accept direct computer output. Video disks cannot do that.

But optical disks store digital, computer-compatible information. At this time, there are two developments for optical disks. One is for large volume disks, storing 50,000 to 100,000 images per disk or even per side. The developers of this product anticipate a sales price of $200-500 (at 1982's purchasing power) for 1986-1987. The second is for low cost drives with low volume disks. Mind you, low volume would still be about one gigabyte (one thousand megabytes), or approximately one thousand images. This means that one optical disk would hold four LFFs. By 1986 such a disk is expected to cost approximately $10. At the time of this writing, there are 30 companies involved in the development of optical disk equipment, mainly in the direct read-after-write (DRAW) technology.

The new optical records are completely different from everything records management has been accustomed to. They are laser processed and promise to be much more rigid than the magnetic storage devices previously described. Their density is fascinating, and they promise to be the true successor of paper as the main information carrier. Companies report that dirt will not affect the information, nor does static or magnetic influence.

These records will have several advantages. First, they are very space saving. Thousands of pages can be stored on an optical disk. This will reduce the filing and storage volume dramatically. Second, an optical disk can be addressed and referenced by multiple users from their desks. No physical movement of the information carrier is required. Also, it can be updated, purged, and reorganized in minutes. It can be asked to correlate, reference, and provide all related file data on any one topic. It permits browsing and scanning and helps the user set up a file search trail. It synthesizes and formats selected data, for example, a client's correspondence on contract matters, for quick review. The optical disk provides for integration of various data stored in different departments when stored in conventional ways.

What are the disadvantages? First is a lack of comparison within the media. Instead of comparing pages or looking up a document, we will have only one screen for information retrieval. It can be expected, however, that the computer industry will come up with some device to make this kind of comparison easier. There are also confidentiality problems. Who is entitled to reference the data stored in such a project? How cumbersome is it to overcome security measures? Last is the dependence on technical equipment. When the equipment is down, one realizes again the advantage of media that do not require sophisticated devices for retrieval.

Will the record department look like a huge juke box, where technical devices pull the required disk and insert it into the computer for accessing and processing? Will the records manager be displaced by this kind or other equipment? Chapter 6 addresses this issue.

At the time of this writing, optical disks are being designed for 100,000 images per disk. This high density level will revolutionize record storage systems even more than anticipated. More data are still needed in regard to accessibility and conditions of long-term storage. It will certainly take a good number of years to develop system packages to store and retrieve the requested set of images within a reasonable time.

NOTE

1. Datapro reports on *Word Processing,* Datapro Research Corporation (Delran, N.J.: 1981), pp. WP71-103.

6

THE FUTURE
OF RECORDS
MANAGEMENT

FUTURE TECHNOLOGY AND ITS IMPACT

Records management went through some substantial changes during the twentieth century. Most changes were reactions to changing requirements. For instance, one change was the constant change of new technology and new equipment, which both required and allowed changes in records management. The high time of the drawer cabinet was the 1920s. Lateral filing did not get under way until the late 1950s. Automatic equipment like power files were first offered in the 1950s. Mobile shelving entered the U.S. market in the mid-1960s, and color coding has been available since that same time. Microfilming took off in the mid-1970s when rotary cameras with built-in quality control were first offered. But what happened in the field between 1970 and 1984?

During this exciting time, when satellites and walks on the moon were signs for technological progress, very little happened in the field of records management. Even today, over 200 million metal fasteners are used every year in the United States, in file folders that have the same basic design they had 90 years ago. What happened to the development of file folder technology after the overwhelming introduction of photocopying and substantial increases in paper volume? Some companies tried some 20 or 30 years back to design a fully automated record system that would select file folders, find them, and bring them fully automatically to the requester. After use, the record would be filed again fully automatically.

Unfortunately, none of these attempts was a technological or financial success. Here and there, an automated equipment company would claim that it had linked the mobile shelving or filing system to a computer in order to select records automatically or to deliver them to a work station. But these remain individual attempts. No company is offering at this time a fully automated filing system that selects individual file folders and delivers them to the work station. The piece of equipment closest to that idea is Minitrieve from Supreme, which delivers a box of records to a person sitting in front of the machine. It is a sign of our times and the state of conventional records management that major filing and system companies, like Remington Rand, could not see any future in hard copy system management. This company, after having a hard look at the future, sold its filing division. When looking at alternative technologies most experts agree: records management, as we know it, has no future. The disagreement is not whether paper records will be replaced, but *how* and *when*. Some experts say that the future will be in micrographics, COM, and related technologies; others (including this writer) bet on optical records.

The records management profession is going to be influenced by (1) changes in media and technologies for information management; (2) different equipment requiring different methods; (3) information being stored, handled, and distributed in new ways; and (4) the fact that the new function arising out of these changes will be more important and more respected than the old one.

How will this influence your position as records manager? The present paper records manager will disappear and a new computer records manager will become more important, respected, and influential. This new person, with more influence, more pay, and more clout, could be you—or could be someone else. The choice lies with you: Do you want to adapt and change into the new role? Or do you feel that you don't want to go through all the hassle, that you'd rather let someone else do it?

If you want to be part of this exciting change, at a time when this profession is finally starting out toward goals we all knew had to come, then you have to prepare yourself. Although these changes are obviously in technology, the implementation of new technology ideas is more important. It is a new philosophy describing the ways information governs our decisions and our life. If records managers in the past had control over all information recorded on paper and/or microfilm, they will have more control over new information sources in the future. They will control information recorded in many ways and used much more frequently, sometimes simultaneously throughout the organization. If the records manager was in control of the memory, that is, recorded and stored information, then this memory has been mostly inactive. Active information stayed in offices where it was required; inactive information was sent to the record department. The value of inactive information is obviously lower than that of active information. The new profession will be responsible for making the most important data available to management at the right time. The difference between success or failure, efficiency or inefficiency of an organization, may depend on its ability to retrieve crucial information from available systems for decisions that have to be made in minutes or seconds. The most important tool in office management is information. The department managing the availability and handling of information itself has tremendous importance within an organization.

The major areas a records manager may be involved in are retention, space management, authenticity of recorded information, comprehensiveness of data bases, retrieval schedules, confidentiality of information, and distribution of information. Records managers have substantial contributions to make in each of these areas. The duties in these fields are the same whether the information is stored on paper, on line in the computer, or on magnetic media or disks. By recognizing these coming changes we can start to prepare ourselves for the future.

WHAT TO DO

Facing the reality of changing technology and, as a result, in a changing profession, it will be up to the individual records manager to prepare for the future. We either can shrug our shoulders and say to ourselves, "I am not worried at this point. I'll take it if and when it affects me," or get overly worried that we may lose our jobs tomorrow. None of this is very helpful when we want to prepare ourselves. The records manager reading these lines has two factors working for her or him. The first advantage is the fact that you are facing the future challenge consciously. This is a great advantage over all those who deny future change and/or do not want to prepare themselves for it. The second advantage is the exciting prospect of taking part in this change, that is, being an active part in this revolution in information management and being able to carry its spirit into our work environment. The records manager can introduce new information technology, set up new policies, and help the organization to be more effective through better information systems. We can prepare ourselves for this role in four ways. First, every records manager should actively familiarize herself or himself with new technologies. Second, an aggressive attempt should be made to participate in this new field. Third, new technologies should be implemented with caution, but wherever benefits could be gained for the organization, the records manager should actively pursue and implement new technologies. Fourth, the records manager should stay faithful to old values of the profession and use the ethics during and after the changeover.

The first essential part of this changeover is for the records manager to become familiar with changes in records management technology. This should involve obtaining information from trade magazines, books, sales literature, continuing education seminars, and other sources. You should know everything worthwhile about the records management field, starting with information in the field of microfilm but involving even more information about data processing and related areas. Take an active part in the professional associations (see the list at the back of the book), and attend state and national meetings of your professional association.

But this may not be enough. It is recommended that you also set up a formal program to familiarize yourself with new technologies and their implementation by visiting and analyzing such systems in related organizations. For instance, if you are working for an insurance company and you hear that insurance company A has just established this new system, you should try to contact that insurance company in order to visit the department and see its value for yourself. Of course, many records managers may be limited by a sense of competition between organizations. However, it is worth a try as it will give you the advantage of being able to sit down at a terminal or reader and actually work with the system. Such experience has proven to be much more valuable than sales demonstrations, literature, or theoretical presentations. Depending on your field, you may set aside a program of spending on a regular basis a certain amount of time for such visitation/education programs. For instance, a medical records professional should spend at least one afternoon per month visiting other clinics or hospitals in the area with new microfilm or computer programs.

The next step in preparation is to be aggressive about participation in new programs involving new information technologies.

We have to face the fact that records management has a pretty low image in most organizations.[1] As a consequence management is often tempted to overlook records managers when new systems are planned or implemented. Too often I hear the same story: A couple of boxes are delivered to the records manager's room. After investigation, it is obvious that these are new terminals, which have been selected and purchased for the records department as part of a larger information system. No one from the records department was informed about the new system until the boxes arrived.

Part of the low image of records management stems from the fact that general management, information management, data processing management, and communication management do not realize the qualifications records management has and the substantial contributions it could offer for the design and implementation of any new system. The professional records manager is trained in the application of systematic analysis and scientific control of records and information from their creation through processing, maintenance, protection, and final disposition, regardless of the medium.[2] These qualifications will be needed in the future, even when different technologies and equipment are around. I do not believe, like some authors, that the records management profession "only arose because of confusion caused by excess of paper."[3]

This profession grew historically as an information management science. Only the drastic changes in media and equipment seem to give the impression that records management has nothing to offer. This is unfortunate but true. It may annoy many records managers who like to sit back and wait until they will be invited to participate in the new programs. Except that the invitation may never come. For this reason we should be aggressive in regard to new programs. Aggressive means that we take the initiative to contact various departments and ask what programs are being planned, at what state of planning they are, and whether you can get involved in it.

This may mean that you have to overcome some pride. As a matter of fact, you are reaching out to management saying, "I want to be involved. You will be surprised what I can offer." Experience has shown that records management has also that stigma of being conservative, negative toward new technologies. This is the result of a number of professional factors. First, the data processing profession is usually not an easy one to deal with. Let's face it, all the buzz words of the computer language and the attitude of being the "only messiah in information and records management" have not helped in regard to cooperation between the two areas. Second, the prophets of new technologies have gone overboard historically when forecasting future changes. Records managers have grown weary of forecasts of when paper is going to be obsolete. As we know, even the microfilm industry got stuck and lost its own momentum. Finally, we can acknowledge (with a chuckle) that records management is traditionally a conservative profession, as we "conserve" valuable goods, that is to say, information. Because of these factors it may be particularly hard for the records manager to reach out and overcome pride.

What are some typical applications where we should try to get involved? First, there are computer programs that involve our department. These involve records management or a part of records management, such as reference index, record trace, inventory file program, and record center management program. Second, there are those programs in which we may have been traditionally involved, such as forms design and forms management. Such would be the field of data capture in the future. Third, there are those areas where information is being generated for short- and/or medium-term storage. This may be a word processing operation or any other process of information generation and storage.

The new records manager will be involved not just in the storage of inactive information, but in the storage of all information, including short-, medium-, and long-term storage. All of this may sound good, but you may ask why should the records manager get involved in these issues. Traditional capabilities and values will be required in any setting. Technology, which may change, only affects the tools of information management. In the past, paper and other conventional methods of recording and storing information were the most efficient tools of their time. Computers and new technologies open new avenues for the handling of information. Records management's capabilities of developing criteria for information management will be needed even more with the new technology. Records management varies according to individual needs, organizational structures, and departmental requirements. However, a number of basic functions can be listed: retention policies and management; authenticity of recorded information; standards for recording; confidentiality; comprehensiveness; space management; distribution of information; and management of information flow. These professional duties of records management will be the same in the future. Changes in equipment will only affect these duties to a minor degree.

There are a number of problems that *arise* from unfinished computer systems design and create opportunities for records management. For example, odd-sized forms and reports for which no appropriate filing mechanism is defined, or provided, require the involvement of the records manager. Retention schedules have to be created for new forms and reports. Written procedures have to be created for the manual processing of computer-related forms and reports. Lack of definition and procedure for vital records protection for hard copy, magnetic files, or microfilm records has to be overcome. Adequate documentation and its protection is required for the computer program. In addition, records managers ought to try to improve less than satisfactory results from procedures related to new records created on computer-related equipment due to lack of orientation and in-service education. Less than satisfactory computer output is due to poor quality input. The records manager can help here and can also deal with the challenge of overcoming low morale, which affects both computer and records management goals.[4] To this list I would add the problem of retention for computer output files. In all of these areas, and others, records management can get involved.

Quite often the records manager asks, "Where should I get involved in a computer program, and where do I have to leave it to the systems analyst or data processing manager?" Let us examine an example, a record department that is designing a new reference index. Table 6.1 shows the individual steps to be undertaken.

All the tasks with an asterisk should be under the final authority of the records manager. Of course, there is no harm done by the records manager getting involved in any additional tasks. However, the ones with asterisks are essentials. Others, like the ones marked with a plus sign, should still involve the records manager, but may also involve a systems analyst or data processing professional; however, 51 percent of the decision should be made by the records manager. That means that input should be sought on the subject, but the records manager should retain the final word.

Similar decision rosters can be developed for any design program. Of course, the essential tasks for records management vary according to program, objectives, and individual circumstances.

Even if it is not possible to get involved in major programs, for instance, because the decisions are made somewhere else, there is still plenty of room to start. Have you checked out yet what is being done to the disks of word processing in various departments? How are they stored? How long are they being kept? If word processing equipment is acquired, can disks be exchanged between various equipment and departments? How is confidentiality handled in the computer room? What retention schedules have been established for floppy disks, disk packs, or tapes?

6.1 Designing a Computer System: Where the Records Manager Should Get Involved

Introduction
    x Background description of present system
    x Introductory reasons for introducing computer system
    + References

1. Proposed System Description
    x 1.1 Purpose and function
    x 1.2 Goals and objectives
      1.3 System design approach
      1.4 Users involved (departments, etc)
      1.5 Project guidelines
    x 1.6 Future expansion
    + 1.7 System evaluation
      1.8 Feasibility Study

2. System Flowchart
    Master system flowchart
    Transaction flowchart
    Narrative procedures outlines

3. System Requirements
    +3.1 Input definitions (how, what, terminals, etc.)
    +3.2 Data input forms samples
      3.3 Data input systems description
      3.4 Inquiry definitions
      + 3.4.1 Access points (search categories)
        3.4.2 Inquiry procedure
        3.4.3 Alternate inquiry procedure
        3.4.4 Inquiry summary response system
        3.4.5 Display/modify response system

4. Computer interfaces

5. Output Definition (print-outs, reports, etc.)
    5.1 Scheduled reports
    5.2 Special reports
    5.3 Output models

6. Data Field Definitions and Record Descriptions
    6.1 Master file record description (i.e., patient identifiers)
    6.2 Data element definition (description of character items, etc.)
    6.3 Data element editing and conversion requirements

7. Operating Requirements
  +7.1 System environment
      7.1.1 Hardware
      7.1.2 Software
      7.1.3 Resources
          7.1.3.1 Core
          7.1.3.2 Disk/Tape
          7.1.3.3 On-line
   + 7.1.4 Terminals
    7.2 Performance requirements
      7.2.1 Responsiveness
    + 7.2.2 Frequency of operation
    + 7.2.3 Data accessibility
    + 7.2.4 On-line data retention
      7.2.5 Reliability
    + 7.2.6 Back-up system
          7.2.6.1 Description of back-up system
          7.2.6.2 Updating of back-up system
      7.2.7 Recovery
      7.2.8 Audit
      7.2.9 Security
   7.3 Operational controls
   7.4 Output handling requirements
   7.5 File conversion processing
      7.5.1 Teleprocessing volume
      7.5.2 Batch processing volume
      7.5.3 File conversion volume
    x 7.5.4 Estimated file size
    x 7.5.5 Estimated file growth
  + 7.6 Manpower requirements

8. System cost
   Teleprocessing cost
   Batch reporting cost
   File conversion cost
   On-line disk storage cost (first year or 3 years)

9. Estimated Cost of Present System
   x 9.1 Labor
   x 9.2 Equipment and supplies
   x 9.3 Communications and systems costs
     9.4 Other costs (space, etc.)

10.   Comparison of present costs to computer cost

x = necessary for records manager to make decision.

+ = where records manager should get involved and make 51 percent of decision.

Aggressive participation in the future information management program is the second step toward the involvement of records management in new ways of handling information. The third is the cautious but positive step toward computerization.

When watching industries and organizations attempting to implement new systems, one can see that approaches often fail because of a lack of preparation and a lack of measurable performance objectives. The records management profession can counterbalance with realism. But at the same time one should be ready to convert to a new system when all signs show that desirable performance objectives can be achieved.

Finally, the old values of ethics as they have been developed by professional records management organizations should be preserved and used during and after the conversion to new media.

The future of your job as records manager will depend on your attitude toward the changing environment. There are plenty of opportunities for the new records manager *who is not afraid and welcomes challenges.*

NOTES

1. Charles Schiell, "Records Management—What?" *ARMA Quarterly* 16, no. 4 (October 1982).

2. John C. Gilbert, "Records Managers: Their Importance Is Recognized," *The Office* 95, no. 1 (January 1982).

3. James W. Oberly, "The Information Revolution in Historical Perspective," *ARMA Quarterly* 16, no. 4 (October 1982).

4. Joseph L. Wright, "The Unfinished Symphony," *ARMA Quarterly* (January 1972).

MANUFACTURERS INDEX

All of the following companies offer automated filing systems. The code (Mv) indicates that they also offer vertical mobile shelving; (Ml), lateral mobile shelving.

AUTOMATED FILING SYSTEMS, INCLUDING HARD COPY AND MICROFILM

Access Corporation
4815 Para Drive
Cincinnati, OH 45237
Tel. (513) 242-4220
Automated retrieval systems for cards, microfilm jackets and fiches.

Acme Visible Records, Inc. (Mv)
Crozet, VA 22932
Tel. (804) 823-4351
Automated retrieval systems, also most other hard copy filing equipment.

AM Bruning
2871 Walnut Avenue
Tustin, CA 92680
Tel. (714) 544-9800
Automated microfilm retrieval system.

Bell & Howell, Inc.
857 West State Street
Hartford, WI 53027
Tel. (414) 673-3920
Automated microfilm retrieval system.

Datafile Limited
One Appletree Square, Suite 200
Bloomington, MN 55420
Tel. (612) 854-0838
Computerized record trace system and color coding filing system.

Eastman Kodak
343 State Street
Rochester, NY 14650
Tel. (716) 724-4000
Automated microfilm retrieval system.

Infodetics
1341 South Claudina
Anaheim, CA 92805
Tel. (714) 635-9500
Automated microfilm retrieval system.

Jefsteel
1345 Halsey Street
Ridgewood, NY 11227
Tel. (212) 494-4004
Automated retrieval systems for cards and microfilm.

Kardex Systems, Inc. (Mv)
Marietta, OH 45750
Tel. (614) 374-9300
Automated hard copy retrieval systems
and comprehensive hard copy filing
equipment.

Nuclip Corporation
121 Mount Vernon Street
Boston, MA 02108
Tel. (617) 523-4449
Filing systems, especially NUCLIP fastener.

Photomatrix
2265 Colorado Avenue
Santa Monica, CA 90404
Tel. (213) 828-9585
Automated microfilm retrieval system.

Supreme Equipment & Systems Corporation (MV, Ml)
170 Fifty-third Street
Brooklyn, NY 11232
Tel. (212) 492-7777
Automated hard copy retrieval systems,
comprehensive hard copy storage systems.

TAB Products (Mv)
2690 Hanover Street
Palo Alto, CA 94304
Tel. (415) 493-5790
Record trace system, also comprehensive
hard copy storage systems.

3M
Building 220-9E
3M Center
St. Paul, MN 55144
Tel. (612) 733-7863
Automated microfilm retrieval systems.

Visual Systems Corp.
3000 Town Center, Suite 3204
Southfield, MI 48075
Tel. (313) 354-1100

White Power Files, Inc. (Mv)
50 Bright Avenue
Kenilworth, NJ 07033
Tel. (201) 272-8888
Comprehensive hard copy retrieval systems, automated storage systems.

LATERAL SHELVING INCLUDING MOBILE SHELVING

All of the following companies offer lateral shelving. The code (Ml) indicates that they also offer lateral mobile shelving; and (Mv), vertical mobile shelving.

Ames Color File Corp. (Mv)
12 Park Street
Somerville, MA 02146
Tel. (617) 776-1142

Andrew Wilson Co.
616 Essex Street
Lawrence, MA 01841
Tel. (617) 683-2403

Aurora Steel Products (Mv)
580 South Lake Street
Aurora, IL 60507
Tel. (312) 892-7696

Bankers Box
1789 Norwood Avenue
Itasca, IL 60143
Tel. (312) 893-1600

Borroughs
3002 Burdick Street
Kalamazoo, MI 49007
Tel. (616) 345-2700

Cole Furniture
640 Whiteford Road
York, PA 17405
Tel. (717) 854-1545

Dennison National Company
Box 791
Holyoke, MA 01040
Tel. (413) 539-9811

Denstor (Ml)
Division of Andersen and Assoc.
Farmington, MI
Tel. (313) 476-6500

Dolin (Mv, Ml)
Division of Stacor Corporation
285 Emmett Street
Newark, NJ 07114
Tel. (201) 242-6600

Eagle Sheet Metal
6226 Howard Avenue
Niles, IL 60648
Tel. (312) 967-5600

Esselte Pendaflex
80 Clinton Road
Garden City, NY 11530
Tel. (516) 741-3200

Estey Corporation
Drawer E
Red Bank, NJ 07701
Tel. (201) 542-5000

Globe Weis
P.O. Box 398
Wauseon, OH 43567
Tel. (419) 337-1010

The Hon Co.
Muscatine, IA 52761
Tel. (319) 264-7100

Jeter Systems
1133 West Portage Trail
Akron, OH 44313
Tel. (216) 773-8971

Meilink Safe Co.
1672 Oakwood
Toledo, OH 43607
Tel. (419) 536-4688

M.I.I. Lundia Incorporated (Mv)
600 Capitol Way
Jacksonville, IL 62650
Tel. (217) 243-8585

Mod-Systems
P.O. Box 547
Greer, SC 29651
Tel. (803) 879-3850

Reflector Hardware Corp.—Space Master
   (Mv)
1400 North Twenty-fifth Avenue
Nelrose Park, IL 60160
Tel. (312) 345-2500

Rotascan Retrieval Systems
111 Twin Oaks Drive
Syracuse, NY 13206
Tel. (315) 437-7589

Systems, Mfg.
13 Broad Avenue
Binghamton, NY 13902
Tel. (607) 723-6344

Spacesaver Corporation (Mv)
1450 Jamesville Avenue
Ft. Atkinson, WI 53538
Tel. (414) 563-6362

Tennsco (Ml)
P.O. Box 606
Dickson, TN 37055
Tel. (615) 446-8000

United Business Equipment
97 Stone Street
Buffalo, NY 14212
Tel. (716) 893-2722

Wenner Business Systems
170 State Street
Los Altos, CA 94022
Tel. (415) 941-2480

Wright Line
160 Gold Star Boulevard
Worcester, MA 01606
Tel. (413) 852-4300

APPENDIX B

PROFESSIONAL PUBLICATIONS AND ASSOCIATIONS

PUBLICATIONS

The following federal publications are available from the Government Printing Office, Washington, DC 20402:

Computer Output Microfilm, No. 022-002-00036-8, 1975.

Information Retrieval, No. 7610-042-8762, 1972.

Microfilming Records, No. 022-001-00056-6, 1974.

Microfilm Retrieval Equipment, No. 022-002-00034-1, 1974.

The following are periodicals in the field of records management:

Administrative Management. Available by writing Administrative Management, Geyer-McAllister Printing Co., 51 Madison Avenue, New York, NY 10010.

American Archivist. Available by writing Society of American Archivists, 300 S. Wells, Suite 810, Chicago, IL 60606.

Information and Records Management. Available by writing to Information and Records Management, 250 Fulton Road, Hempstead, NY 11550.

Journal. Available by writing American Medical Record Association, 875 N. Michigan Avenue, Suite 1850, Chicago, IL 60611.

Journal of Micrographics. Available by writing NMA National Micrographics Association, 8728 Colesville Road, Silver Springs, MD 20910.

Modern Office Procedures. Available by writing Industrial Publishing Co., 614 Superior Avenue West, Cleveland, OH 44113.

Records Management Quarterly. Available by writing Association of Records Managers and Administrators, P.O. Box 8540, Prairie Village, KS 66208.

The Office. Available by writing Office Publications, Inc., 1200 Summer Street, Stamford, CT 06904.

Today's Office. Available by writing Today's Office, P.O. Box 619, Garden City, NY 11530.

PROFESSIONAL ASSOCIATIONS

American Management Association
The American Management Association Building
135 West Fiftieth Street, New York, NY 10020
Tel. (212) 586-8100

American Medical Record Association
875 North Michigan Avenue, Suite 1850, Chicago, IL 60611
Tel. (312) 787-2672

American National Standards Institute
1430 Broadway, New York, NY 10018
Tel. (212) 354-3300

Association of Records Managers and Administrators, Inc.
4200 Somerset, Suite 215, Prairie Village, KS 66208
Tel. (913) 341-3808

Institute for Certified Records Managers
P.O. Box 89, Washington, DC 20044

National Micrographics Association
8728 Colesville Road, Silver Spring, MD 20910
Tel. (301) 587-8202

Society of American Archivists
330 South Wells, Suite 810, Chicago, IL 60606
Tel. (312) 922-0140

APPENDIX C

RECOMMENDED READING

ARMA. *Bibliography on Records Management*, 1980. Available from the Association of Records Managers and Administrators, P.O. Box 281, Bradford, R.I. 02808.

ARMA. *Correspondence Course*, 1970. Available from the Association of Records Managers and Administrators, P.O. Box 281, Bradford, R.I. 02808.

Johnson, Mina M., and Norman F. Kallaus. *Records Management*. 2nd ed. Cincinnati: South-Western, 1972.

Maedkae, Wilmer; Mary F. Robek; and Gerald F. Brown. *Information and Records Management*. Beverly Hills, Calif.: Glencoe Press, 1974.

Neuner, John J. W.; B. Lewis Keeling; and Norman F. Kallaus. *Administrative Office Management*. 7th ed. Cincinnati: South-Western, 1978.

NMA. *Bibliography of Micrographics*. Available from NMA: The Image Processing Association, 8719 Colesville Road, Silver Springs, Md. 20910.

Quible, Zane K. *Introduction to Administrative Office Management*. Cambridge, Mass.: Winthrop, 1975.

Terry, George R. *Office Management and Control*. 7th ed. Homewood, Ill.: Richard D. Irwin, 1975.

Weaver, Barbara N., and Wiley L. Bishop. *The Corporate Memory*. New York: Wiley, 1974.

INDEX

About the Author

C. PETER WAEGEMANN is Executive Director of the Institute for Medical Record Economics, Inc., a non-profit organization in Boston, Massachusetts. He was previously President of Herbert Zippel (UK) Ltd., a British-German manufacturer of filing systems and computer supplies, and Vice President of Ames Color File Corporation in Massachusetts. He is an inventor and has published articles in *Physicians' Management, Computers and Health Care, The Imaging Administrator,* and the British edition of *Hospitals.*